Introduction to Dramatherapy

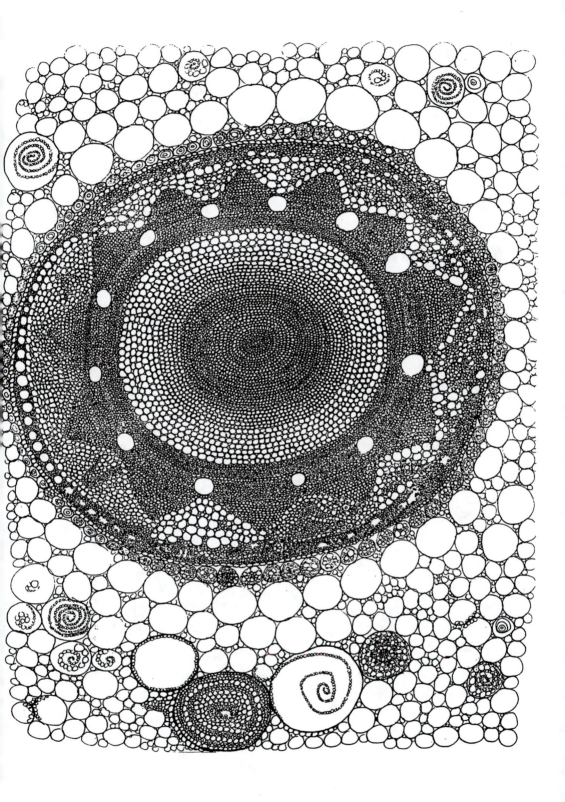

Introduction to Dramatherapy
Theatre and Healing
Ariadne's Ball of Thread

Sue Jennings

Foreword by Claire Higgins

Jessica Kingsley Publishers
London and New York

First published in the United Kingdom in 1998
by Jessica Kingsley Publishers Ltd
116 Pentonville Road
London N1 9JB, England
and
29 West 35th Street, 10th fl.
New York, NY 10001-2299, USA

www.jkp.com

Copyright © 1998 Sue Emmy Jennings
Foreword Copyright © 1998 Claire Higgins
Printed digitally since 2004

Library of Congress Cataloging in Publication Data
A CIP catalog record for this book is available from the Library of Congress

British Library Cataloguing in Publication Data
Jennings, Sue
Introduction to Dramatherapy
I. Title
616.891523

ISBN 1 85302 115 6

Contents

Foreword

I met Sue Jennings in 1989 when she was organizing the first Dramatherapy and Shakespeare Symposium in Stratford-upon-Avon and I was playing Titania in *A Midsummer Night's Dream* and Gertrude in *Hamlet* with the Royal Shakespeare Company. Within five minutes of our beginning our discussion I felt an enormous excitement about what she was saying. My understanding of what I was trying to do in the theatre as an actress took an immediate and quantum leap. Sue was talking about direct experience in theatre and dramatherapy in a way that cut cleanly across the boundaries erected between the two, and thereby introduced me to a whole new world of possibilities of my own work.

In our respective ongoing journeys we have repeatedly sensed how empowering and natural the meeting of these worlds is, despite the sometimes uncomfortable process involved in challenging preconceptions and long-held beliefs of other professionals in the field of theatre and therapy. In our shared experience of taking theatre into Broadmoor, for example, we confirmed with joy that our worlds did indeed cross over, and in the meeting place, new ways of working were forged.

Sue's knowledge that the theatre of healing is a real place, not a theory or a principle, gave me permission to view my own work in an utterly different way, and to acknowledge the feedback I was directly experiencing from audiences wanting to be allowed to know theatre as a healing place, rather than an intellectual, academic and often rather puzzling and unsatisfying experience.

I am extremely grateful to Sue for opening up the immense possibilities of our work, for her great generosity with ideas and her commitment to the belief that, because the act of theatre requires a witness, the present destructive emphasis of society on the individual becomes, in the theatre of healing, the individual in context, ie, working/being with others. For me this is truly why dramatherapy is a 'therapy of optimism', as this book describes; a therapy that does not simply reach back endlessly into our individual pasts for clues to the present, but states now, in the immediacy of the present, our hopes, fears, needs, desires, thereby weaving us a direct thread to our collective future, as well as our past.

As you take hold of the thread of this book, I hope your journey is as exciting and fruitful as mine continues to be.

Clare Higgins
Glastonbury

To Mooli Lahad with affection, for many years of working
and playing together through stories and dramas
in UK and Israel.

What is Dramatherapy?

Dramatherapy is the application of theatre art in clinical, remedial and community settings with people who are troubled or unwell.

Whereas theatre art could be termed preventative in relation to mental health, dramatherapy is curative.

Theatre art is necessary as a transformative medium for people both as individuals and groups to maintain optimism, higher awareness, and find resolutions. Dramatherapy is necessary in exactly the same way, as a transformative medium for people who are clinically ill, damaged or vulnerable.

Dramatherapy methods include movement, voice, dance, theatre games, role play, improvization, text work, puppets and masks. Indeed, all skills from theatre are selectively applied with client groups to enable verbal and non-verbal expression and resolution within a dramatic or story structure.

Dramatherapists work in diverse contexts which include: psychiatric hospitals and day-centres, special schools, GP surgeries, community centres, prisons and probation service, as well as private practice.

Dramatherapists at one of the six recognized courses in the UK have formal post-graduate training and their practice is closely monitored through regular supervision by their professional body, The British Association for Dramatherapists. Dramatherapists are also conducting masters and doctoral research.

Dramatherapy is now a State Registered profession and is regulated by the codes of ethics and practice of the British Association for Dramatherapists and the standards demanded by the Council for Professions Supplementary to Medicine (CPSM).

Ariadne and Theseus

Most accounts of the story emphasize the valour of Theseus in the slaying of the Minotaur with brief mention of Ariadne, as in this account from *Gods and Heroes of Ancient Greece* (Hollinghurst 1973).

Minos was king of the island of Crete and his son had been killed by a fire-breathing bull at Marathon near Athens. In payment for this, each year Minos had demanded tribute of seven boys and seven girls from Athens – and fed them to the Minotaur, a creature with a bull's head and the body of a man. When the demand for tribute came again, Theseus volunteered to go as one of the boys.

When Theseus reached Crete, Minos' daughter, Ariadne, fell in love with him and said she would help him if he promised to marry her and take her to Athens. The Minotaur lived in a labyrinth, a maze of passages and rooms, under the palace at Cnossos in Crete. Ariadne gave Theseus a ball of thread, which he could unwind as he made his way through the labyrinth, and a sword so that he could kill the Minotaur and then follow the thread back to the opening. Thus armed Theseus went down into the labyrinth.

Meanwhile, in the innermost chamber of the labyrinth, the Minotaur slept. His man's body, huge and muscular, was stretched out on a slab of rock; the fierce head, with all its black curls and matted fur, lay quite motionless, except when a nostril quivered or a great ear twitched.

The very sight of young Theseus was enough to enrage the Minotaur; he lowered his horns, and with a force that no man had ever yet resisted, he charged down on the enemy. Theseus leapt to one side, and the Minotaur, stumbling, felt the sharp stab of a sword as it entered his flesh.

Theseus escaped from Crete with Ariadne but, when they put in at the island of Naxos on their way to Athens, the god Dionysus claimed Ariadne for himself and Theseus left Naxos without her. Theseus had arranged with his father Aegeus that if successful, he would hoist a white sail instead of the black one used as a sign of mourning when the tribute ship departed and returned. Theseus, however, forgot to hoist the white sail and Aegeus, who was watching for the ship from the cliffs and caught sight of a black sail, threw himself down into the sea, which was called Aegean after him.

Theseus became King of Athens, unified the surrounding villages into a single state and was afterwards honoured as the founder of this state of Attica which was later to grow into the Athenian Empire.

In fact Ariadne was betrayed and abandoned by Theseus on Naxos. The following is from *Who's Who In The Ancient World* (Radice 1971), where she is described as an inspiration to writers, artists and musicians – very similar to Shakespeare's Ophelia.

Ariadne

The daughter of Minos king of Crete, who guided Theseus through the labyrinth by means of a ball of thread so that he could escape after killing the Minotaur. He took her away with him but abandoned her on the island of Dia (later identified with Naxos). There she was found by Dionysus (Bacchus) who married her and gave her a crown of seven stars which became a constellation after her death. Ariadne's betrayal by the ungrateful Theseus is one of the themes of Catullus's longest poem (64) and she is a natural subject for one of Ovid's romantic *Heroides*, which accounts for her appearance in Chaucer's *Legend of Good Women*.

She was also well known to Hellenistic writers and artists. The statue known as the 'Sleeping Ariadne' in Rome is copied from a Hellenistic original. But though she could express for Catullus his personal sufferings in love, for the Renaissance she became more a symbol of life through death because she was gathered up into the divine ecstasy brought by Bacchus. His arrival was painted by Titian in his *Bacchanal* (which Poussin copied) and in *Bacchus and Ariadne;* Tintoretto and Raphael also painted Ariadne and her divine lover. This concept was revived in the opera *Ariadne auf Naxos* by Hugo von Hofmannsthal and Richard Strauss, where the classical story is the play within the play; Ariadne abandons herself to death only to find new life in the god.

So many of the Greek Gods and their stories as well as the ancient Greek plays are an inspiration and structure for dramatherapy work. From this story alone we also have the adventures of Theseus and his near death at the hands of Medea; his meeting with Oedipus when he welcomed him to Athens.

Dionysus, of course, is one of the gods of theatre art who in balance with Apollo ensures the presence of both the chaos as well as the order, the dark as well as the light, the revelry as well as the restraint.

However, it is Ariadne the guide and support to Theseus in his confrontation with the Minotaur and who is later abandoned, who has particular resonance for dramatherapists and performers. We will remember the ball of string which can guide us through the dramatherapy maze and hold an image of Ariadne as our personal guide through this book.

Tributes and Challenges

I have not written this book as a researched investigation of all theories and practices pertinent to the field of dramatherapy. Rather it is my own statement and personal philosophy of how I see and experience dramatherapy and theatre of healing. It would be impossible to separate out every nuance that has been influenced by others. I wish to give tribute to as many people as I am aware of, who by their writings, thoughts and discussions, have shaped my understanding of dramatherapy. First and foremost I must of course mention Peter Slade for being who he is, and his pioneering endeavours in the world of Child Drama. His influence has been profound both on drama teachers and dramatherapists, as well as other pioneers at the time: Gavin Bolton, Richard Courtney, Dorothy Heathcote, Veronica Sherborne, Brian Way.

However I do not wish to mention just those people who have stimulated me or who happen to agree with me. There are many people over the years who have challenged, fought and disagreed with what I have said and done, who have equally enabled me to clarify my ideas or to rethink my position.

Of course students, trainees and clients must have the biggest tribute and there should be a special mention of trainees and staff in Greece and Israel. As the founder member, with Gordon Wiseman, of what is now the British Association for Dramatherapists, I have learned so much by being in at the beginning, taking office for many years, editing the *Dramatherapy* journal, being placed outside at the margins and then being re-incorporated as an elder, with perhaps a little wisdom.

As the initiator of dramatherapy diploma training at St Albans College of Art and Design (now University of Hertfordshire), and the College of Ripon and York, and later the founder of The Institute of Dramatherapy (now at The Roehampton Institute) the various struggles with personalities and institutions are legion. However it was always interesting to both myself and Billie Lindqvist who founded Sesame (now at Central School of Speech and Drama), that everyone else's struggles were projected into our relationship. Billie and I have disagreed about many things, especially during the formative years, but we hold a strong mutual respect for our differences and are always stimulated when we manage to meet and talk.

It has seemed important not only to develop appropriate training for dramatherapists but also to discover a language of dramatherapy that has its own coherence and identity. This is an organic process and courses and ideas change and grow. They meet new needs and situations and are constantly being tested. People seem to think that I mind when changes take place and new discoveries are made. I should be very concerned if things did not change. If dramatherapy becomes set in stone, then indeed that will be its death-knell. We only have to look at the history of theatre in its many forms and structures – some connected and some appearing like a tree on a once-barren landscape – to see how art, especially theatre art, grows, changes and transforms. The arts change as society changes; and sometimes art follows culture and at other times anticipates it. And in my view, dramatherapy is derived from theatre art and is therefore able to transform our experience and perception of the world.

Theatre friends and colleagues over the years have always revitalized me; from supportive encounters, especially towards healing theatre with people like Alan Badel, Julie Christie and Glenda Jackson in the early years, my close friendship with Harry Andrews who died too early, as did Flora Robson, to the energy and insight of those I work with now, notably Clare Higgins, Joan Walker and Andrew Wade.

Over the last four decades – yes I did my very first dramatherapy in a clinical setting at the age of 17 – I am sure I have offended many and confused even more, especially those involved in my earliest work, which was experimental. However, many survived the experience and have remained long-term colleagues and friends. I especially want to mention Gordon Wiseman and later Jane Puddy, David Powley, Ann Cattanach, Alida Gersie who have not always agreed with me, but I love them dearly. In the new generation of dramatherapists, former students or supervisees, including Marina Jenkyns, Steve Mitchell, John Casson, Anna Chesner and Phil Jones, have survived my conceit and found their own particular directions with an occasional backward glance.

People like Murray Cox and Don Feasey have also been intellectual combatants, especially over questions concerning the relationship between dramatherapy and psychotherapy. The exchange has always been useful and I know we all acknowledge our own particular expertise. It was sad for me when Don was unable, because of illness, to write a chapter in *Dramatherapy*

Theory and Practice 3. Murray and I always found our meeting in Shakespeare even though we might walk contrasting paths. Indeed the five Shakespeare Symposia, 1989–1993 in Stratford-upon-Avon, were the place where my dreams of Theatre and Therapy came together into a living present through Shakespeare. Actors, clinicians and dramatherapists met in a vital way to explore practically a Theatre of Health and Healing. Mark Rylance and Clare Higgins made very powerful impacts both in *Hamlet* and at the first Symposium. I feel proud that I introduced them to Murray Cox and then became part of their unique Broadmoor and Shakespeare collaboration. It is indeed tragic that just as this book was completed, Murray Cox died suddenly and unexpectedly. Murray and Alice Theilgaard have both contributed generously to dramatherapy thinking.

Many performers contributed including David Bradley, David Calder, Jeffry Dench, Kate Duchene, Ralph Fiennes, Susan Fleetwood, Debra Gillett, Patrick Godfrey, Clare Holman, Peter de Jersey, Christopher Luscombe, Mike Maloney, Josette Bushell Mingo, Amanda Root, Michael Siberry, Robert Stephens, Susan-Jane Tanner, Andrew Wade, and they reminded those present that dramatherapy has to exist in proximity to the theatre as we addressed the current plays of each year; 1989 *Hamlet, A Midsummer Night's Dream,* 1990 *Much Ado about Nothing, Troilus and Cressida,* 1991 *Henry IV ii, Two Gentlemen of Verona,* 1992 *As You Like It, The Beggar's Opera,* 1993 *The Merchant of Venice, Venetian Twins.* The debate and discourse between theatre and therapy was truly enriched by all the participants as well as the productions.

More recently I have been excited and challenged by working with Katie Mitchell, Juliet Stephenson, Nigel Cooke and Debra Gillet and been reminded how important Beckett is, when wrestling to understand the human condition.

My family and friends may not always be close but are always there for me in times of need and indulgence. My grandchildren are a constant source of inspiration for my life and work. There are some special friends I must mention by name, Clare Higgins, Audrey Hillyar, Robert Landy, Åse Minde, Galila Oren, Margaret Orr, Suzanne Reading, Katerina Robertson, Robert Silman, Andrew Wade, Joan Walker.

However I must own and take responsibility for my conclusions.

Introduction to the Dramatherapy Maze

First take a ball of string to guide your way into the maze of your imagination. Remember to attach it to the door lintel; unravel it as you go. Maybe Ariadne, your co-dramatist, will hold the end firmly, as you go through a journey of exploration and transformation.

In the story of Ariadne it was thought that the **monster** was at the centre of the maze. Dramatherapy and Theatre have themselves been considered monstrous and dangerous. We are going to conquer the dramatherapy monster.

So far as I know, this is the first time that an attempt has been made to write an interactive book on dramatherapy; a book which keeps the reader 'in the frame' or perhaps 'on the stage' as part of the process. I try to place the reader at the heart of the drama throughout this book, but in particular through the questions and exercises at the end of each chapter This book is about your own dramatic experience, and I hope that through that experience you will understand something about the world of drama and therefore dramatherapy. I use the word `dramatic' to describe the episodes that have been interactive, rather than those that have been headline news. Because people understand things better from their own lived experience, I am sure people will have a greater clarity about dramatherapy when they relate it to their own life experience and journeys, both in the present as well as the past. As the writer, I too am putting myself 'on the stage' and will record my own dramatherapy development in relation to the dramas and theatricality of my own life.

Some of the experiences you will be writing down or reflecting upon may not, at first, seem like dramas at all and I am asking you to take on trust the journey on which we are both about to embark. We shall both be taking risks and perhaps my risks, as the writer, will be more public than yours as the reader. However, it is a good idea if you have a companion for this journey and I suggest that you have a co-dramatist, your Ariadne who will guide your journey and with whom you can share your memories and reflections. There are examples in several chapters that would be enhanced by you and your co-dramatist enacting the scene or the story. If there is a small group of people who can all follow the journey together, it will assist you all to maximize the experiences that you discover. You may choose someone, before you start to answer the questions, with whom you can process your responses. If you prefer to work by yourself, then acknowledge the guide within you, your own personal Ariadne; otherwise note the questions as you move through the book. It is your choice.

Drama, theatre and thereby dramatherapy are in themselves interactive processes that involve other people, so it is important that we reflect on our history not just as individuals but as *individuals in relation to other people*, in other words, the community. The current trend of much therapy as well as of society itself is towards the cult of the individual, often at the cost of other people. I discuss this in more detail later but think it is important for us to be aware of the swing towards the idea that healing has to happen in a clinic rather than allowing that it could well be more effective in the community.

However, as you are reading and recording throughout this book, it is important to remember that Theatre Art cannot function in isolation; it is the only art form that actually needs other people or at least one witness to the drama being enacted on the stage. However much we may feel that others in our past life have troubled us, how can we find any resolutions if the other players are not present?

In a psychodrama group, which is a very particular form of theatre, we may well have these other people represented and their roles may be acted out by ourselves or by other members of the group. This enactment relies solely on our own memory and version of the events. The story may well take another turn as we respond spontaneously in the drama, and we may find through an upsurge of emotion, triggered by a memory of an event or phrase or image, that we feel a post-cathartic relaxation. It is similar in its totality to post-coital relaxation, though both may be tinged with a touch of depression. We may also feel that we have found a solution or even THE solution. This I think is where the theoretical basis of psychodrama is flawed and I will discuss this issue of 'solutions' and 'reasons' and 'causes' later, within the context of psychotherapy.

When we witness a drama as a piece of theatre, we are in a different kind of space-set-apart, watching or participating in an enacted event whether it is a clear narrative or not, where the total piece is much larger than ourselves or our own personal story. We become drawn into a spectacle within which we may have significance but are not the totality. Thus theatre art enables us to find our place in a symbolic enacted world, as part of a story that will present us with various choices and solutions; it will transform our experience. It is rather like looking through a kaleidoscope and shaking all the bits of coloured paper to form new shapes and patterns without losing its essential form. Because we have been habituated to certain acts of drama from a young age, we are able to transpose ourselves into a piece of theatre and live through it, as a member of the audience; we do not necessarily need to be a participating actor. This having been said, when I discuss the application of dramatherapy I shall demonstrate the importance of the therapeutic effect of stepping onto the stage of healing theatre. It is important to remember that the theatre experience enables us to go beyond ourselves into experiences that I think are metaphysical; the reality that is theatre not only takes us out of our own day-to-day existence, but also shifts how we perceive and cluster our views of life itself. People always need to ask questions about their place in the world in their search for meaning; it is a part of being a person. These questions can gain greater clarity when we are involved in the active transforming medium of theatre art. We organize and structure our lives in dramatic form and, indeed, I suggest that drama and theatre are the driving forces of human behaviour and communication.

I hope that these early chapters of this book, together with the experience you have thought about or will have written down and processed in parallel with reading, will give you some idea of the breadth and depth possible from the dramatherapy journey and that you will be able to make links with your own experiences and the core concepts of dramatherapy. These are:

1. Theatrical distance

2. Everyday reality and dramatic reality

3. Embodiment–projection–role developmental paradigm (EPR)

4. Dramatic reworking of experience

5. Dramatic structure of the mind

6. Ritualization of life events

7. Expansion of roles and transformation

8. Lived metaphysical experience.

This book is an invitation to the reader to discover more about dramatherapy and how the application of theatre art in special situations can improve people's lives. Theatre in itself can be healing when it transports people away from their everyday lives into stories and scenes on the stage played out by actors. It is the actors' job to communicate through created and fictional characters in a structure that has a beginning, middle and end; the very structure of a play, whether it has a narrative or is a stream of consciousness, nevertheless creates form around content.

Many people have less experience of live theatre and more of film and television, and many theatre pieces rely heavily on technology. However, technology is not necessary to take us to a different place and time; all we need is a special space set apart, a good story and one or more performers who can enact that story. Although I do not want to negate the importance of film and television, I feel it is important to understand how live theatre interacts with us as live people in the audience. In this live interaction, we respond both as individuals and as a collective group. We are not only transported into a different reality, or the experience would be purely escapism, we are also presented with relationships, conflicts, themes and outcomes which touch our own lives. We therefore usually leave the theatre with new thoughts and ideas, feelings of resolution, and the experience of transformation. For this to occur, it is necessary for the experience to be dramatically distanced from our own lives, so that we are not just seeing a replication of our conflict. Rather we are witnesses to a piece of theatre taking place in distanced time and space which enables us both to see something more clearly, and to understand it in new ways, and also to enter it without risk and therefore to come closer to it. This journey through a dramatic structure peopled by actors is made both by ourselves and with others, and reaches a conclusion, even though this may only be temporary. This is the healing journey of live theatre, and dramatherapy is based on the application of this healing theatre with people who are troubled.

This basic introduction to dramatherapy is for a reader coming from any profession – indeed from life itself, to help them make some sense of the importance of theatre as a healing experience. Readers will be invited to consider their own dramatic development and thus demonstrate to themselves the importance of drama and theatre. Some of the information is based on my personal and professional experience and the stimulus I have received from my family, students, colleagues and clients alike. Much of the stimulus has been a challenge to try and clarify my own thinking and ideas; at other times it has been to help me illuminate what I am trying to talk about. Again it has proved an enormous help to me when family and friends have helped me keep my feet on the ground by reminding me of the ordinary when I have been tempted to leap into the extraordinary!

I am saddened when dramatherapy appears, at times, to have become yet another competitive battleground for originality and point scoring or when it threatens to be subsumed by other disciplines. Attempts to standardize the dramatherapy experience will fail, as repressive attempts to limit the remit of theatre have failed. However, whenever our creativity is restricted, it will find a new way of being. I am reminded of the time when theatre was banned during the English Interregnum and it immediately went underground; even the tennis courts of the wealthy were quietly loaned for theatrical presentations. In earlier generations when theatre was thrown out of the churches it immediately became vibrant on the streets. Any attempts to institutionalize it will produce a counter-culture rather than controlling its capacity to subvert.

Nevertheless I am also gladdened to see that dramatherapy can have such a profound influence and be all encompassing. It is now 'accepted' as a means of treatment with vulnerable populations and has status in government departments, notably the Department of Health. However we must be vigilant. The fields of education and therapy are very volatile; training courses are re-writing themselves, and the aims and intentions of therapy are being re-evaluated. Let us not lose the very artistic freedom that is at the core of dramatherapy in an attempt to impose conformity. Of course we need to have standards, and to develop research and find ways of evaluating what we do. Very often it is the groups themselves who experience dramatherapy that will do this for us. When I facilitated a dramatherapy project at Broadmoor Hospital based on the story of the Odyssey, it was the patient and staff discourse that held the key to evaluating its success. Similarly with the first Broadmoor programme I conducted through *A Midsummer Night's Dream*, a whole battery of tests demonstrated the development of individual patients; but it was the group sculpting that showed the improvement in patient and staff communication and trust. It was the risk-taking in the drama that enabled the improvement of morale on the ward.

Business plans and the purchaser provider economy have brought about a swift change in the selling of dramatherapy. Can we sell it in terms of employability? In terms of success stories? In terms of it being attractive sounding? In terms of it providing a personal development for the trainee? It terms of it *mattering for humanity and the future*? Perhaps my strongest concern in the continuing debate is that a community of people can create something that matters to them.

Most people who have trained as dramatherapists, whether or not they go on to practise as dramatherapists, usually describe having experienced a profound transformation of their lives. No-one undertakes a course from a neutral stance and although dramatherapy training courses are not offered as personal therapy for the students, this is just what it becomes both for the individual student as well as for the group and the tutors. The importance of the theoretical as well as the experiential course content means that students can move in and out of the experience while their own issues are being addressed within the dramas.

I have been asked why all people who do a dramatherapy training do not go on to practice it, and I do not think it is to do with problems of employment. My view is that many people, through the dramatherapy training, get to a point where they can make informed decisions about their lives; they come to various crossroads on their dramatherapy journey and consider the implications of taking a particular turning.

Dramatherapy training is as much a rehearsal for living as it is an apprenticeship for a profession. Where else can we take risks, create, put our ideas and feelings into dramatic form, consider human issues through play texts and novels, become more adept through movement, voice-work, acting? The advantage of doing a dramatherapy training as contrasted with an actor's training is that there can be greater understanding of the processes involved rather than just the techniques and products. However, it is important that dramatherapy training has enough emphasis on the necessary skills, which should include not only voice, movement, improvization, text and mask work, but also technical knowledge of lighting and effects, prop and costume making, stage management and stage directing. I wish all dramatherapy courses were able to include this technical knowledge, perhaps by having a placement at a theatre.

There is only one dramatherapy course, to my knowledge that actually teaches stage directing and this was at the request of the senior psychiatrist, who thought the students were being taught too much pathology. He had seen the effects and outcomes of dramatherapy on groups of in-patients with severe mental health problems and realized that dramatherapy could offer something unique. He felt that the dramatherapy should have more theatre structure rather than less. His junior colleagues were not quite so convinced and wanted a pathology focused treatment programme rather than an artistically drama focused programme.

I shall discuss in more detail my ideas on the training of dramatherapists. I have a certain sympathy with this psychiatrist who has identified an issue in dramatherapy training where psychology is being taught at the expense of theatre art or where dramatherapy is being seen as a form of psychotherapy rather than as an artistic therapy.

After all this debate, we shall be influenced by what we think will benefit ourselves and our friends and families. As society becomes more affluent, and our first considerations are not food and shelter, what else do we need? Or should the question be, what else do we desire?

It would seem that the desire for drama does not correlate with hunger and shelter needs. Even if we are on the poverty line, we still want or need to participate in ritual celebrations and group dramas and theatrical events. Perhaps a cautionary tale at this point illustrates my point.

In my own religious development I have been a member of more than one belief system. Like many people I was striving after truth and meaning, (a good friend said to me recently, perhaps if I strove less the truth would come through!). Some years ago I was attending what was supposed to be the most special event on the Christian calendar: Midnight Mass at Christmas – the first Holy Communion of Christmas Day. I have attended many of these celebrations in many cultures and always anticipate the time when it will be truly 'meaningful'. This particular year there was a reasonable solemnity and jollity and a few good choruses of 'O Little Town of Bethlehem', 'Once in Royal David's City', interspersed with bible readings; one or two strained looking parents wondering if they would again get questioned about virginity and offspring of the womb. So far so good. It was time for the sermon. The bishop was giving the sermon and surprise, surprise, his theme was the 'true meaning of Christmas'. In his attempts to explain the true spirit of giving, he vilified what he saw as the worst example of stupidity he had witnessed. He described to us with much gesticulation, a single mother, and a black single mother at that, who had sold her furniture in order to buy Christmas presents for her children. He sounded as if he was describing the worst possible sinner, and at Christmas too. Surely I am not the only one to think of this mother who wished to celebrate Christmas and therefore sold her only assets, as being quite a remarkable person. She knew the importance of the ritual and celebration that is the drama of Christmas, which had to take precedence over the basic comforts of her own life. Yet she became the outcast and the castigated – and became them at Christmas of all times! If we stand back from this particular woman's story, we can also begin to understand how symbolic and ritualistic acts can be misinterpreted as everyday actions. We shall discuss the differences between the everyday reality of our mundane experience and the dramatic reality of our symbolic experience later. No matter how impoverished we are, we have a basic need for the creative experience and the artistic expression. Theatre and ritual are essential for survival and allow us to develop not only as individuals but as communal groups; not only physically and mentally but spiritually as well. How else can we develop a conscience about our actions, if not through the experience of being 'other' as well as 'self'. Instant expression does not lead to responsibility for outcome and thus a sense of conscience.

Our attitudes to theatre art, and therefore to dramatherapy, are influenced by what actually matters to us, our families and our futures. What I intend to demonstrate in this book is that dramatherapy and theatre have crucial parts to play in the survival of the species, indeed the dramatic act itself may well be biologically determined, and be the starting point for the cultural dimension. I shall start by inviting you, the reader, to tell your own story of your dramatic history, from as far back as you can recall, with prompts, if possible, from other people in your life; from memories, recollections, hopes and fantasies; from celebrations, rituals and rites of passage; with favourite songs, games and dances; and day-dream, dreams, imaginary friends and imagined roles; and of course with special moments from visits to the theatre and other performances, best-loved stories, myths and legends.

These are just snatches of the multiplicity of experiences that make up our dramatic experience from birth to death or, more accurately, from womb to tomb. It may surprise you to know that the drama commences *in utero,* when our mothers create imaginary dramas with us, before we actually exist independently; and the dramas continue after we have died as those who are still alive have conversations with us for many many years. Maybe when we consult a medium to contact someone who has died, we do not trust our own dramatic capacity to continue our imagined relationships. Many people continue their dialogue with their dead loved ones without needing the intervention of a medium. In some societies, ancestor worship is established as a religion, rather than as an individual's response to a dead relative, friend or colleague; and talking to people who have died and interpreting their wishes for us, is incorporated into the belief system of particular cultures.

Already I hope that your perception might be stretched in terms of what is dramatic and how intimately it is woven into your own life and experience and of those with whom you are in contact. Furthermore, the reader will begin to follow my line of reasoning that society itself is theatre-centred, indeed *we construe our lives in dramatic form*. We only need to recall the last time that we re-toldsome event that happened to us to realize that we told the story in dramatic form, playing out the roles and scenes for whoever is listening. We remember and describe our lives as dramatic scenes with a beginning, middle and an end, where characters interact with one another.

Finally, in this introduction, I have to point out that much of dramatherapy is woman centred. Since women are the guardians of so much of our dramatic experience, we must acknowledge their central role in a theatre-centred society. I describe in subsequent chapters the importance of the dramatic interaction between pregnant women and unborn children as well as mothers and young children. If we look at the historical role of women and healing we can observe how often they are the keeper of stories that are passed from generation to generation. Even though Shakespeare was a man, the mouthpieces of the women in his plays are a strong centre of wisdom and healing.

For example, the following speech of Titania in *A Midsummer Night's Dream* illustrates the illness, chaos and loss of art and play that ensues when the spirit world is at war, when a sense of conscience has been lost.

These are the forgeries of jealousy;
And never since the middle summer's spring
Met we on hill, in dale, forest, or mead,
By paved fountain or by rushy brook,
Or in the beached margent of the sea
To dance our ringlets to the whistling wind,
But with thy brawls thou hast disturbed our sport.
Therefore the winds, piping to us in vain,
As in revenge have sucked up from the sea
Contagious fogs which, falling in the land,
Hath every pelting river made so proud
That they have overborne their continents.
The ox hath therefore stretched his yoke in vain,
The ploughman lost his sweat, and the green corn
Hath rotted ere his youth attained a beard.
The fold stands empty in the drowned field

And crows are fatted with the murrion flock.
The nine men's morris is filled up with mud,
And the quaint mazes in the wanton green
For lack of tread are indistinguishable.
The human mortals want their winter cheer.
No night is now with hymn or carol blessed.
Therefore the moon, the governess of floods,
Pale in her anger, washes all the air,
That rheumatic diseases do abound;
And thorough this distemperature we see
The seasons alter; hoary-headed frosts
Fall in the fresh lap of the crimson rose,
And on old Hiems' thin and icy crown
An odorous chaplet of sweet summer buds
Is as in mockery set. The spring, the summer,
The chiding autumn, angry winter change
Their wonted liveries, and the mazed world
By their increase now knows not which is which.
And this same progeny of evils
Comes from our debate, from our dissension.
We are their parents and original.

A Midsummer Night's Dream Act II, Scene 1, lines 81–117

Women have pioneered healing and scientific roles in an essentially male dominated world, and we need to remember that many women were punished by men with the rise of western medicine. They were punished for being very successful healers and midwives and it is not accidental that a strong content of my own theatre work has been the presentation of the stories of these very women who were killed and castigated for their achievements.

A very reassuring creation story for me, is the tale told by the Temiars in Malaysia where the founder was an old midwife who dreamed and tranced the world into being. Dreaming and trancing are two activities intimately connected with ritual and theatre where there is an altered state of consciousness together with an artistic form. Perhaps we neglect the times when we 'are not ourselves' and for women this is especially at menstrual times, pregnancy and the post-partum period. Of course I know that there are hormonal and other physiological changes; nevertheless we know that the act of drama can actually bring about a physiological change. The drama can pre-empt the physical rather than it merely being the physical that causes the drama. There will be more such discussions throughout the book.

It is time to move into our first chapter which addresses the question `Why Drama and Dramatherapy?'

Exercise

Consider the following questions. You can write down the answers, note them in your mind or come back to them in more detail later.

Your current experience – now!

1. Write down as many words as you can, that relate to your experience of the words DRAMA and THEATRE. (Give yourself 3 minutes for this.)

2. Underline with a colour those words that have a negative feel about them, and use another colour to underline those words that have a positive feel.

3. Count up how many positives and how many negatives and write the two numbers in the right hand margin (e.g. 5n, 6p).

Place this on one side to compare with other attitudes later on when you have completed the more detailed questionnaires.

CHAPTER ONE

Why Drama and Dramatherapy?
'Finding the thread'

Dramatherapy is the term used for the application of theatre art in special situations, with the intention that it will be therapeutic, healing or beneficial to the participants.

This is my own personal definition and refers to the totality of the drama and theatre experience, rather than to elements of it.

Some definitions refer to 'drama providing tools in dramatherapy' or the 'elements in drama being applied to therapeutic process'. Drama and theatre are far greater than the sum of their parts and my definition refers to **theatre and drama as healing processes**, whether or not they are applied with a therapeutic aim or intention.

Within the overarching or underpinning main aim of dramatherapy, there will be various more specific aims such as: enabling communication, stimulating new thinking, providing means of resolution, developing new skills, transforming unhelpful experiences, looking at choices, enacting new journeys, understanding gender issues, exploring politics and so on.

Dramatherapy is primarily an artistic therapy which gives opportunities for expanding our perceptions and understanding of the world through witnessing the drama in the world of the theatre; maybe we can understand the globe by going to The Globe. Many theatres are named after famous theatrical people (Olivier, Gielgud), royalty (Prince of Wales, Queens) place names (Old Vic, Aldwych) or else after mythic symbols (Apollo, Mermaid, Pit), statements about great people or great symbols.

Dramatherapy has had to address many prejudices and many people assume that drama and theatre are luxuries and nothing to do with the real business of living. Drama is marginalized in many schools, theatre groups close down and funding is always the major issue for keeping live theatre alive. We also have attitudes towards actors: we both love and hate them; we enjoy their stories in the tabloids but we also expect their stories to be there. There is still a feeling that actors are vagabonds who are lacking in morals, and do not deserve to be paid for what they enjoy doing.

These prejudices are backed up in all sorts of ways, even for young children. I was re-watching the Disney version of *Pinnochio* with my grandchildren recently and sang along when Pinnochio goes off with the actors – the fox and the cat, 'Hi diddly-dee an actor's life for me'. What I had not recalled was the next scene where Jiminy Cricket, who plays Pinnochio's conscience, is trying to get Pinnochio away from the actors and is ignored; Jiminy turns his back and says, 'O well, what does an actor want with a conscience anyway'.

Dramatherapy as part of theatre art needs to be understood principally through theatre theory taken together with cultural concepts. We need to place theatre back in the centre of human development and experience and not necessarily process it through theories and ideas from psychotherapy.

One of the main objectives of this book is to demonstrate how we weaken the power of dramatherapy by diluting it with too much psychological theory or psychotherapeutic analysis, whereas we strengthen it by keeping it firmly in the frame or stage of theatre art. There are attempts to explain dramatherapy with psychoanalytic interpretations or to see our dramatic development as part of our psychological development.

There is also the suggestion and even belief that artistic expression is a substitute for sexual activity; that sexual impulses are sublimated through the arts. I wonder if the reverse is actually the case: that sexual activity can become a substitute for artistic expression. If we do not have sufficient artistic dimension in our lives, maybe we seek recourse in a sexual substitute. Theatre art in particular can be a frightening process, especially when it moves us from self to other, and makes us confront the outcome of our actions. We should ask ourselves whether we avoid confronting the self by merging into sexual release.

Theatre art in its various manifestations including ritual performance, is a potent force in society. It has existed through time despite major antithetical forces which have included both religious and economic factors. Thus it follows that dramatherapy as an intrinsic part of theatre art is a most potent form of therapeutic intervention and exists in its own right with its own theory and practice. Indeed the word theory – *theoria* comes from the same root as the Greek word for theatre – *theatron*. The ancient Greeks knew that we could understand something more clearly by seeing its enactment at the theatre, and indeed were well aware of theatre both as entertainment and as a form of healing.

The more we are exposed to theatre art, the more skilled we become in being able to communicate in dramatic form about our experiences. I have observed a tendency in dramatherapy groups for participants to rush into an improvization and complete it very quickly. They are often reluctant to stay with the artistic process. Then they are amazed where the journey takes them if they continue. Repetition of art takes us into greater depth. I suggest that from birth we are able to respond dramatically to the world around us, and that during the early years we are both player and playwright in the way we start to construe our perception of the world. If this aspect of ourselves is allowed to develop we become more adept at dramatic construction and it is enhanced and enlarged by our increasing imagination. Our imagination is essentially dramatic in nature as we remember and recount not necessarily events that are 'dramatic' in themselves but rather, we dramatise them as a way of communicating them. Placing them in dramatic form means that they are manageable and containable and that we can communicate the events to others.

Although dramatherapy may be practised as an individual therapy, its most effective practice is with communities of people. If I work with individuals in dramatherapy, it is purely as a means of enabling them to make a transition into a group, in other words, a community. My concern with the practice of too much individual therapy is discussed below in my critique of psychotherapy.

Dramatherapy may be practised by some as an active psychotherapy, although as I have already said, I believe that this reduces its effectiveness. If it is practised as a psychotherapy it means that the process itself has to be analyzed and interpreted. It may well bring the process to a halt and the creative energies that were being enabled through the drama experience have to be re-kindled. It can be compared with constantly starting a car and not driving off or continuous foreplay without sexual union. As a colleague once said to me: just stay on the train and stop jumping off to examine the undercarriage!

However, we live in a climate of counselling being prescribed for every type of stress, and long term psychotherapy or psychoanalysis being looked upon as desirable. Talking about myself is seen as 'a good thing' and a lot of people earn their living by listening to people talking about themselves. Many others mortgage their lives to pay for being listened to. There is no television programme about any kind of distress that does not have an accompanying helpline, and public disasters attract professional carers on the next aeroplane. There is no pause to see if an individual or a community may have their own self healing resources.

Maybe this sounds very harsh but I do have concerns. I wonder if counselling or psychotherapy are always the most effective forms of instant intervention, especially when the potential for intrinsic healing within the community is ignored.

Psychoanalysis and other analytic forms of psychotherapy are still unproven forms of therapy, and much of psychoanalytic theory stands only if one is prepared to make a leap of faith. This is not without irony since psychoanalysis itself was anti-religion, yet set itself up as a 'messianic' movement with disciples and a code of belief. People who did not 'believe' were cast out of the movement or recommended for more analysis to explain their 'avoidance'. Let me illustrate this with a recent personal experience.

Two colleagues and I intended to stage a London fringe revival of Nicholas Wright's play, *Mrs Klein*, and we had cast the play, booked the venue, and agreed the performance rights. Unfortunately the rights were withdrawn because of the new contract for the New York production (we were somewhat flattered that we were seen as competition); however, before they were withdrawn, we had budgeted the costs of the production and a major part of the funding was being raised through workshops. We planned dramatherapy workshops that would not only explore key themes in the play itself such as the relationship between Melanie Klein and her daughter and son, but also examine key issues in Kleinian theory such as her ideas of child development. One workshop was called '*child as monster, child as saint*' which would look at the stereotypic projections we put onto babies and children. These projections are similar to those we put onto people from other cultures, especially cultures dissimilar from our own in physical appearance, practices and beliefs. It is interesting the xenophobia that has become apparent about joining Europe; suddenly, other Europeans are so dissimilar that collaboration means alien invasion. The idea that Europe can be a *community* seems intolerable. Dramatherapy for Brussels please!

I use these workshops frequently where dramatherapy is used to explore key issues, through the text of a play or the text of a theory. For example in

Israel during the last ten years, a group of twenty or more professional people come together for two days in a space set apart. To date our exploration have included: *A Midsummer Night's Dream, Hamlet, King Lear, Oedipus* (Theban Legends), *The Odyssey, The Good Person of Sezuan,* Dreams and Dreaming, Visions from the Old Testament, Nature and Healing.

I saw no reason to suppose that an exploration of Mrs Klein the woman and her practice would be any different from the workshops that I had been facilitating for years. However, the outrage from traditional Kleinians took us by surprise, as if we had great audacity to even contemplate the idea. Yet by comparison, the Old Testament workshops in Israel were welcomed by the most traditional of Jews even when they took place on the Sabbath. Surely our knowledge is strengthened by being explored and challenged rather than being stated as givens, especially when the givens have not necessarily had objective scrutiny.

Psychoanalysis has permeated so much of our thinking and there are psychoanalytic dissections of many art forms, paintings and even Shakespeare's plays. Both Freudian and Jungian approaches as well as some of the newer generalist 'object relations theories', attach reductionist meanings to observed phenomena. This 'meaning', if it is never challenged, becomes a closed system of thought, a *reduction* of understanding. The difference with dramatherapy is that it allows an *expansion* of meaning together with choices.

The Oedipus myth is reduced in psychoanalysis to two scenes (killing of father and marrying of mother), which are extrapolated and applied to all human development. The rest of the story is ignored. As one cynic pointed out to me, you could say that the killing at the cross roads of an old man by Oedipus, (he later realized it was his father) is an early example of road rage! The insistence on these events as central to boy's development, is an example of mythic distortion, to reinforce a patriarchal view of society. Most small children develop strong parental attachment which is influenced by the parent they play with more. The dramatic play ensures healthy relationships. If we isolate certain observations and call them Oedipal we de-contextualize children's experiences. If we impose adult interpretations, we produce a self-fulfilling prophecy; a prophecy that is de-contextualized from the ancient Greek story.

The drama development of young children, the movement through embodiment, projection, role (EPR), gives a framework for observing their play within which their struggles, attachments and core stories are enacted.

We are all born dramatized and through the dramatic imagination we could speculate on an idea like 'Oedipal development'; but let us not confuse it with everyday, observable reality and insist we have a theory.

The prime factor in relationships with one or two parents is that of dependence; babies and small children are dependent on adults far longer than other animal species. As a child approaches teens there is a struggle to be independent from parents and to rely more on the peer group. This is hard for humans since biological maturity is in advance of the economic reality of independent living. In my view it is quite pointless keeping young people at school and trying to make them learn something when they have no engagement at all with what is being taught. Children are kept at school, not just because it is supposed to be good for them to learn things but also because there is nothing else for them to do and no money to keep them at home. Having won some degree of independence from parents and other adults, what then can this energy be used for? Young people are struggling with a society that cannot for artificial reasons respond to their needs. No wonder it is a time of rebellion.

Successful therapy in my frame of reference is therapy that places me in a context not only with other people but also in scenarios and landscapes that are significant in the world. I am merely a small part of the totality and the welfare of the human species is surely as important as my own welfare. Therefore therapy which focuses on me being able to talk about myself, increases my self-centredness and narcissism.

If I stay at the centre of my universe rather then being aware of others, and thus part of a community, in other words, socialized, I am unable to be aware of others unless I am able to be 'the other', something which the act of drama makes possible. Indeed, my thoughts, feelings and actions need to be regulated by my conscience which means I need to understand the implications of my actions; **I need to be aware of outcome before any action is taken**.

However, if I believe that I am at the centre of my universe and that my personal world takes precedent over the worlds of others and the world as a whole, then self is the motivation for my thinking and doing. Thus my experience is severely impoverished since it only resolves around myself. Motivation of self cannot exist without motivation of others and I need to be other in order to enhance my own understanding. The dramatic impulse 'as if' means that I have some understanding of the life of another person and am able to develop a connection with and empathy for that person. Theatre is a collective representation of a story that draws me into the experience and I am able to make connections with and feel for the other characters in the drama.

I also have concerns that psychoanalysis relies upon verbal exposition. The body is kept as still as possible while either in a prone or sitting position and words are the main content of the analysis. Some non-verbal cues may be considered such as postures and gestures, but words are considered the symbols to bring about understanding of an individual's 'inner life', usually described as their intra-psychic world.

However, all animals, including human ones, are constantly in action; stillness merely highlights the actions that follow; even in sleep we are unable to be still for very long. Our bodies lead all our activity and over the years are trained and developed to service the various practical and creative tasks in which we are engaged. However much we may be taught about the economical use of movement to achieve a task, the creative impulse to make it varied is always rippling under the surface. When someone describes an event to us, our body responds in fear, or revulsion or warmth or recognition as we dramatize the event in our imagination. We think dramatically about the world, which means our dramatic imagination is constantly recreating the scenes and events that are being told to us.

The dramatic development of the human body is a constant theme throughout this book and will be discussed in more detail. It is important here to underline the importance of bodily movement in relation to the differences between dramatherapy and verbal psychotherapies. Human movement is sometimes interpreted as 'acting out' when it occurs in verbal therapy yet I find it extremely difficult to understand something or even recall things if I am sitting or lying down. We can observe very small infants spontaneously moving in rhythm on the one hand and exploring new movements on the other. They are repeating rhythmic movements that give pleasure as well as experiencing the unexpected joyously and excitedly. We derive both pleasure and excitement from the combination of the things that we know and the things that are new and this forms the basis of much of our life and theatre experience. I have referred to it as the 'ritual and risk' of our structuring of life experiences.

Even the writing of this book is interspersed with regular bouts of movement, pacing, dancing, walks round the block, hand rubbing, swinging or rocking in my chair, foot tapping, and also imagining the things that I am writing about. If I start to feel drowsy then I need more vigorous movement together with an increase in fluid intake, a complete pause away from the manuscript. I perform repetitive movements such as pacing up and down as well as unexpected movements such as hair pulling. I am physically involved in the writing of the book, even though the main activity of writing is a projective one. Writing a book (or any act of writing) is, in the main, a projective activity, where thoughts, feelings and ideas are recorded outside of the human body. Other projective activities can include: painting, drawing, doodling, clay work, and the dramatherapy techniques of 'sculpting'.

I may school myself to be economical with the use of my body, especially in crowded social situations, cramped space, or in times of illness when energy needs to be conserved, to give but a few examples. I may have learnt to cower at a raised hand or a raised voice or learnt that little girls do not kick their legs in the air or had my energy channelled into socially acceptable activities like gymnastics and tennis. Society has conventions about what is acceptable for me to do with my body, despite the increase of freedom in recent years. Girls are still admonished if they display violent behaviour similar to men's violent behaviour. Furthermore they are punished more severely since women are not supposed to be violent, and men's violence can be 'understood'.

In my personal experience, long periods of physical inaction make me lethargic, unfocused, destructive and uncreative. It is the same when I sleep; I actually sleep for short periods, and used to be called an insomniac. 'You should do something about it' I was told, 'Perhaps you should see a therapist'. For a time I accepted this view and felt that I 'ought' to be sleeping for longer periods, but it just did not make sense. I wasn't feeling tired or dropping off to sleep in the daytime or not completing tasks that I ought to complete. I thought back to my own childhood which I describe in more detail later, and remembered that I had never slept for long periods. Although I was born in an era when children were sent to bed early, I never used to sleep; I would read, write, compose, listen to the grown-ups as I sat on the stairs. I would go to sleep around the time that the adults members of the family slept, and I would usually get up before them in the morning. I realized that my bouts of wakefulness coincided with some of my most creative times, that I feel none the worse for them and indeed they are the means of focusing my energy. My most negative experiences have been during brief, thankfully infrequent, bouts of illness which have been serious enough to immobilize me.

It could be argued that my own personal view of psychotherapy is not enough on which to build a critique and I would be the first to agree. However, I have worked in dramatherapy with many people for whom the verbal approach has not worked and who have sought something different after years of 'trying'. Psychotherapy can be very seductive when people are told that they are 'avoiding' or 'defending' or 'repressing' if they do not feel that the therapy is working. People who are already very vulnerable are susceptible to the persuasions of some therapists and some religions alike and need some consumer protection.

Most people still do not have access to consumer guidelines for finding a counsellor or psychotherapist. Many psychotherapists are discomforted when clients ask them for their qualifications or ask if they can assess the therapist as well as being assessed themselves. Some psychotherapists insist clients take holidays at the same time (or else pay for the sessions when they choose to take their holidays at a different time); that missed sessions for illness or crisis are paid for even if due notice is given. I know clients who have to pace the pavement outside their therapist's house because they do not have a waiting room. This encourages control by the psychotherapist and dependency by the client.

People have come to see me for dramatherapy for whom the building up of their self-esteem took priority over the many issues they thought they needed to deal with. Their experience of psychotherapy had exacerbated the low self-esteem they already had, as a perpetual search for childhood explanations yielded solutions that had meaning for the psychotherapist and not for themselves. Yet in dramatherapy they were able to participate in a series of role building sessions where they took on new roles rather than repeating old ones, and journeyed through new landscapes rather than staying stuck in old cycles. Their achievements in the dramatherapy overcame the lack of self-esteem and the new skills in body and voice provided the means to express a new confidence.

Dramatherapy is a therapy of optimism; it is a therapy of now and the future; it is able to assist people to move on, rather than perpetually delve into an unhelpful past.

Much psychotherapy says that the past holds the key to an unhappy present, and people are encouraged to regress to earlier times to remember forgotten or repressed experiences. I am convinced that much of what we forget is forgotten for good reason. Some of our forgetting is a practical necessity, otherwise we would just overload; some of the information is just in abeyance, until such time as we need the information. For some experiences, however, forgetting is a healing process and helps us deal with material that should be forgotten for its horror, terror or destruction or just because it is unhelpful. I think that being able to forget is probably a biological survival mechanism and is one way of processing material that is not useful to us. Through the dramatic experience we can recreate a world that is more satisfactory and feel that we can influence our future rather than being tied to our past. Our past has gone and cannot be changed. The only thing that can be changed is our current attitude to our past, especially if it involves burdens of guilt and shame. There are however, some things in our life that we do need to feel guilt and shame about; all of us have done things that we wish we had not. The only way forward is to learn from these experiences rather than indulge in them.

This is particularly the case when our memories are so fickle. If we ask several members of the same family about a certain event they will all give a differing perception. Research has shown that people can imagine a past event when no such event took place. Some psychotherapists maintain that clients reclaim their past. However there is great unease about the false memory syndrome, especially as it is being applied in relation to the many selves that we inhabit both in our past as well as in the present. It is very easy to re-create a past and believe in it, especially when a present is unsatisfactory. Similarly, a group of people see a play and will all bring away a variation in experience; when there has been an accident different people will notice different details.

In therapy one is creating a fictive situation which may have some elements of truth in it. Any event once happened is turned into fiction through memory and sometimes it may be a totally false memory, based on a dramatic leap of the imagination. On the other hand, experiencing new forms of my present life might well change things in a more profound way, and I suggest that this can be achieved through theatre art. I think this applies to all major distress and especially for those people suffering from 'post traumatic stress disorder'.

If we have experienced a severe trauma, the reliving of it as a form of exorcism has not been found to be helpful to many people, and in many cases they have not been able to thrive. Sudden single trauma is destructive because it is often a random experience and usually destabilizes us. We therefore need the sort of therapy that can help us rediscover stability and find our place in the world again. We need to rediscover meaning in our lives and to feel that the world is not an unjust place. We need to re-establish our identity without feeling the guilt of being the survivor. None of this is helped by re-running and repeating the experiences, which often happens to people in flashbacks and nightmares. We need to ritualize the experience and move on to rediscovery of stability and belief. By ritualizing the trauma, either by telling it or creating a symbolic drama, it allows forward movement rather than repetition It is then possible to deal with the after effects such as loss of belief and confidence. In dramatherapy, of course, this is possible and the following example illustrates my point.

I was facilitating a dramatherapy workshop in Israel, in the desert known as the Negev. It was during the time that an Israeli soldier was being held captive and very complex negotiations were taking place for his release. In the refreshment breaks on the course, there was a lot of discussion about the incident and although many sons and husbands had been killed in the wars, this one soldier seemed to symbolize them all.

On the second day of the workshop, it was announced on the news that the soldier had been shot. It spread round the group like wildfire and many participants broke down and wept. People came to me to say that the workshop should be cancelled, that it could not continue in the circumstances, that it would be wrong to continue with *drama* when such a *real experience* had touched everyone's lives.

I assembled the whole group. There were some thirty people, and everyone shared their immediate feelings of grief, despair, anger, fury, impotence and loss. People were screaming, sobbing and keening. Someone suggested that we should now cancel the group and go home, 'losing this young man is like losing my own son' and someone else said 'I have lost my son in the war'. Again someone said that this was a real experience, a real loss, and we should not be doing 'just drama'.

I suggested that perhaps we could make use of the drama to pay tribute to all these losses as well as the immediate loss of the young soldier. The group looked puzzled and unconvinced, and it was now that I really felt some doubts about not being Jewish. How could I really understand? I was also getting caught up in reality and drama. I went on to suggest that we could devise between us all a requiem for the dead soldier. The group agreed to try and I proposed that each of the small groups went for a walk in the desert to be with their own thoughts and that they brought back anything they thought might be appropriate to help create the ritual. The walk in nature had a very calming effect and people brought back rocks and desert flowers and branches and fossils as well as discarded rubbish. Each group created a landscape and from that made a ritual of movement, music and voice as their acknowledgement of what had happened. At the end the whole group came together, singing and moving. It was not a tidy, well made presentation but it provided a structure to both contain and express the strong thoughts and feelings in a dramatized form; not just sadness was expressed but fury and futility as well. Although it had a structure, its chaotic moments mirrored the chaos of people's experience about the war and its implications. It provided some dramatic distance without denying the feelings and it enabled the participants then to move on to further dramatherapy work and thus complete their course.

My overall understanding of dramatherapy has come from being able to observe dramatic phenomena in a wide range of cultures and situations, as well as my own theatrical and therapeutic life. I have not observed just theatre performances but religious rituals, rites of passage, the dramatic playing of small children, and the drama of institutions - hospitals, universities, political arenas. My investigative journey has taken me to many countries and even when I have been side-tracked into other explanations and interpretations, I have always returned to a *theatrical structure of society and a dramatic structure of the human being.* We organize our lives in theatre form and we respond to society with scenes in our dramatic imagination. The dramatic imagination is what will enable us to survive. The fact that we can imagine another, and therefore imagine outcomes and consequences of what we do, illustrates that drama is essential for shaping our social behaviour. It fosters both communication and co-operation; it provides role-models and outcome management.

We go to the theatre to see the issues of life played out in front of us, and we also respond in our lives with what we have learned through our dramatic imagination. Life and theatre are distinct and I do not wish to blur the boundaries; it is those boundaries that enable therapy and growth to take place. Nevertheless what we learn in one sphere can carry over into the other and my everyday experience can feed my imagination just as my imagination can feed my everyday experience. When as a child I learn things from my mother, part of that learning is through her 'role-model' – in other words she models appropriate behaviour for me and I will usually simulate what she does. However, that is not all that happens, when my mother is role modelling, I am also imagining myself as a mother, as a grown up; I project myself into the future and see myself playing out a role not dissimilar from hers. If I grow dissatisfied with her model, then I start to imagine myself behaving in a different way. I project myself into the future and see myself in those situations, where I take on a variety of roles and relationships.

My dramatic imagination helps me deal with my present and prepares me for the future and allows me to develop empathy and a conscience about my actions and their effect on other people. I achieve this because the nature of human thought is essentially dramatic and has been developed as such from an early age. When I do go to the theatre or watch films and television, I am transported out of my own imagination and transported into a larger world, where I can find my place within the larger story. I am not limited merely by my own experience but can expand my perception of both myself and others in the world.

I have stated my conviction, perhaps rather forcefully, that I see dramatherapy being a primary therapy as well as seeing drama and theatre as the basis of human action. I have discussed how we organize our lives and our imaginations in dramatic form as well as suggesting that we need theatrical experiences in order to develop in a healthy and responsible way. These themes will be further elaborated upon as we journey through this book.

Barney: We're going to play lions.

Harry: Come on Barney, let's take our clothes off.

Mum: Why are you taking your clothes off to play lions?

Barney: Lions don't wear clothes.

The two boys aged 3 and 3½ roared and giggled for an hour and then put their clothes back on again.

Exercises

You can write the answers or create drawings or doodles – respond in whatever way seems right.

These questions are about the dramas in your past. Whatever your age now, make sure you respond to stages in the past.

Young adulthood (18–25 years) or adulthood (26 years plus)

1.   Write down any experience of being in a drama group/class. Describe the activities and whether it was a positive or negative experience.

2.   Describe any particular experiences of going to a live theatre, and any 'special moments' that you can recall from specific plays.

3.   Describe any particular experience of going to live theatre that was a negative experience.

4.   Can you recall, in your adult life, any other experiences that could be called 'drama'? Having to do 'role-plays'? Getting up to speak in front of an audience? Please describe and comment on whether they were positive or negative.

Teens (12–17 years)

5.   Did you 'do' drama at school? Describe whether you did it as a subject or as part of English or as an end of term activity or as an option. Describe the activities and performances/projects that you were involved in and whether they were positive and/or negative.

6.   Did you attend drama classes outside of school? If you did, please describe.

7.   Did you go to the live theatre? Describe any special moments or any experiences that were negative.

Young times (7–11 years)

8. Did you belong to a drama club or class? Describe what you did and what you thought about it.

9. Were you taken to the live theatre, perhaps for a seasonal or birthday treat? Describe what you can remember and what you thought about it.

The above questions make fairly conventional assumptions about the nature of drama and theatre and although we may have been taken to see a pantomime or been in the nativity play at a younger age (if so, please write down about the experience), we do not usually think about drama experience beginning until at least seven years old. We may, however, use the term play instead of drama for earlier activities. You may also have memories of other people's attitudes towards these activities; maybe it was 'in' to be in the drama group or maybe it was the opposite; maybe your family did not approve of you doing drama (did you have to study more seriously?) Can you recall genderized attitudes towards dramatic activities that you have engaged in; for example, were you encouraged to only take very 'feminine' or 'masculine' roles?

CHAPTER TWO

Drama at the Centre and Drama at the Margins
'Threading our way through'

GRANDMOTHERS

(By an eight-year-old boy)

A grandmother is a woman who has no children of her own, and therefore she loves the boys and girls of other people. Grandmothers have nothing to do. They have only got to be there. If they take us for a walk they go slowly past beautiful leaves and caterpillars. They never say 'Come along quickly' or 'Hurry up for goodness sake'. They are usually fat, but not too fat to tie up our shoe strings. They wear spectacles and sometimes they can take out their teeth. They can answer every question, for instance why dogs hate cats and why God is not married. When they read to us they do not leave out anything and they do not mind if it is always the same story. Everyone should try to have a grandmother, specially those who have no television. Grandmothers are the only grown-ups who always have time.

Now that we have begun to consider our own dramatic development, and you the reader are thinking about the drama journey in your own life, let us now consider the evidence of, and consequence for the embededness of the drama in our lives. We shall consider the imagined play in pregnancy right through to the developmental play of children, where the basis for dramatic interaction is being laid; where perhaps the most important foundations of all are being built.

'I'm not me any more – I am being taken over by another; as the baby grows I have to make sure there is still room for me. I keep telling the baby to wait a bit, I'm not ready!'

The pregnant woman who said this was not resentful in any way but was very much aware of the change in her identity now that she was 'one plus another' as she used to describe it. Perhaps we are now more surprised at the new feelings when we are pregnant; our family life style is less ritualized and patterns of parenthood have been disrupted. Although we have more scientific knowledge about maternity, it does not necessarily help us deal with the overwhelming feelings often experienced by pregnant women.

However, the most important illustration of the above quotation is the conversation about this imagined other. The 'baby' already exists as a person in the imagination of the mother, and causes the woman to have feelings of displacement, and she reports having a conversation with the foetus. This is an example of the early dramatization before the child is born. We shall see from further examples that mothers are at the very centre of children's early dramatic development.

The drama has already started *in utero* when dramatic interactions take place between the mother and her unborn child. This appears to be the core of our early dramatic inheritance.

For many years I thought that the 'dramatic experience' started shortly after an infant was born. Dramatic 'engagement' was stimulated and reinforced during the first year of life. With my recent observations of pregnant women and babies I have revised this view; I now realize that the first dramatic interaction is usually set up between pregnant women and their unborn children. A women talks to the imagined child, sings to it, asks it questions, and then she answers herself AS IF she is the child. It is such a simple everyday occurrence that I had not even noticed it. You may challenge my notion that this is a dramatic interaction. However, if you observe pregnant women talking in this way you will see that they are 'in role', using a different voice from their everyday communication; they reverse roles with the imagined child, as they answer themselves.

'In role' as mother and infant, the communication is often accompanied by movement and gesture such as rocking, stroking, patting and finger play; and the gestures change depending who is speaking. A dialogue takes place with the mother taking both roles, using a dramatic convention of change in voice and movement in an imagined context, usually in a space set apart.

> Esther: (*stroking her belly*) 'Now little man – I shouldn't say that should I – well little person – how come you are nice and quiet today; (*patting her belly strongly; as the child*) Oh well Mum, I'm only having a rest, you wait 'til later, (*as herself*), I know you little rascal, you'll want to start leaping about just when I want to have a rest.'

I have noticed an increase in these conversations once the foetus begins to move about, and the conversations spiral to some frequency once the kicking is stronger, especially at antisocial hours. Fathers too, if they are awakened by sudden bursts of activity start to have these imagined conversations. Early in the pregnancy, mothers often have anxious conversations if there has been no movement, and the imagined child is imbued with many characteristics while still *in utero*.

> Rosie: (*hitting her belly*) 'Are you still there? You'd better be – for God's sake move; please please move; just a little kick; what are you trying to tell me? (*As child*) I'm going to be a lazy old slob like Grandad. (*As herself*) And cheeky with it I'll bet – oh there you go – now don't overdo it.'

From observations and discussion, it would seem that women talk in this way reasonably frequently, that is, several times a week, whereas men do it occasionally, especially when a particular aspect of the imagined infant has struck their attention.

> Mike : (*to Molly*) 'I suppose we should be putting his name down.'

> Molly: (*to Mike*) 'For a school? Let's at least wait until IT'S born. Don't bank on it being he.'

> Mike: (*in reply*) 'For the football team of course – and you can't tell me it's not a lad with kicks like that (*places hand on belly and sees it thrown away with delight; to foetus*). There's my boy, strong as an ox already aren't you? (*As the foetus*) that's right Dad – I shall be in the team before I can walk!' (*Peels of laughter from both father and mother.*)

These examples illustrate the dramatic act which includes both a change of voice and role reversal. The mother does not talk to the embryo in her usual voice but in a voice for the imagined child; she then reverses roles with the child as she answers herself. This is an act of drama for it stems purely from the dramatic imagination of the mother, and may well encompass the hopes, fears and ambivalence of the mother to her unborn child. I have observed this type of dialogue not only with pregnant women but also with women experiencing difficulties conceiving, as they talk with not the *imagined child* but the *imaginary child*.

> Charlotte: (*hugging her belly*) 'Oh where are you? Do you think you might be there – can you answer me and let me know – I really want you and love you.'

Women contemplating termination of pregnancy may also talk in this way; for example I have heard them apologise to the unborn child.

> Susie: (*rubbing her hand over her belly and up and down her legs*) 'I really am sorry – I just can't have you at the moment – it just can't happen – you've come too soon – one day...'

It would seem that many women across many cultures talk to the embryo or foetus in this way and role reverse *as if* they were talking as the child. This imaginary conversation must be the earliest possible example of dramatic interaction in the life of an infant and one has to ask why this happens? Women have commented that they have not liked to admit they do it, that people will think they are crazy or stupid,

> Norma: 'You won't tell anyone – I'm sure people would think there was something funny about me – I'm sure other people don't do it – but it feels cosy to have a little chat and tell it secrets – like I used to talk to my Mum after she died.'

People have also commented that they talk in a similar way to their pets, especially dogs, and that one of the most frustrating things about keeping a parrot was that it mimicked rather than answered.

> Pat: 'I talk to my dog – I don't have children – but the dog answers me – I feel a bit stupid really – but I ask the dog something and then answer myself – we have long

conversations when we're out in the park – I don't know what people must think!.'

It would seem that humans talk in the dramatic convention and role reverse without being taught and thus my speculation is whether this is necessary for human society to survive, both as individuals and as groups.

As an individual, if I am able to play at both self and other, does this strengthen and affirm my developing identity? Because I can role reverse with another, does this enable the development of empathy and through empathy bring about awareness of outcome and thus conscience? Is understanding of 'other' a biological necessity for the species to continue because we need the group to survive?

Once the child is born there is a continuation of the dramatic interactions between infant and mother or other carer. Conversations through facial expression, sound and words take place and the infant will both echo and also initiate. The much debated smile response is usually accepted now as a smile rather than wind! These rhythmic sound interactions, which are very similar to those initiated by the mother during pregnancy, take place for as long as the mother has time, patience and inclination. The early months of the infant demonstrate childlike humour and resilience and determination to seek solutions.

Sadly this energy can be channelled into inappropriate directions through too early-age technology, and also through neglect or abuse. It is essential during this early time that the imagination is stimulated through the senses and that this playing is interactive with the adult.

During the first year the infant by and large is responding through sensory and bodily means. Variations in sound, light, taste, touch and smell are major transitions for the child. For example, a change of place can be helped by the blanket or shawl remaining the same, or a change from breast feeding to bottle feeding can be helped by bottle feeding with breast milk. Infants respond to the way in which they are held or not held, and to their own body in relation to the immediate physical world around them. It is a world of proximity both in time and space where the physical presence of other is essential.

Babies that tolerate long periods alone without searching for responses from others are often depressed rather than being 'good' or 'no trouble'. Babies are 'trouble' because they continue to insist on interacting with others, the essential communication in dramatic form, which appears to have as much priority as the satisfaction of other sensory requirements. The paradox of the attachment to the mother during this time is that there is also room for dramatized distance, for example when there is friendly struggling, rolling and pushing. The infant's body on the one hand is co-operating with the mother as they rock and cradle together; but it is also resisting against the mother as they struggle and wrestle. There is a paradox here that sometimes the struggling is 'for real' and sometimes it is part of the game; already the child is sorting out different planes of reality.

The first year is very much the time of physical and sensory play and is referred to as *embodiment* (E) or *sensory/physical play* in terms of children's dramatic development.

In the traditional design of a kibbutz in Israel, the children's house is always in the centre and the adolescent house on the margins. Children are seen as needing the protection from any invasion, whereas adolescents are preparing for their transition into adulthood and are allowed to create their own life dramas without interfering with the rest of the population.

The physical presence of the child at the centre and the adolescent at the edge, is also how it is in dramatherapy. The centre of the dramatherapy maze is the child, the inner core of creativity that often gets forgotten on our own life journey's development and only becomes monstrous if it is forgotten.

Towards the end of the first year of life the child is increasingly aware of the outside world and responding to greater distance in time and space. Special toys and bed coverings are invested with strong feelings of attachment and the child is beginning to role reverse with these special objects as the mother did during pregnancy. **The child will talk to teddy and then answer on teddy's behalf.** As the child begins to explore the world outside of the body, much of the playing is still very sensory with the actual feel and texture of sand and water, pastry and so on. However, there is increasing play with toys and stuff, often rubbish too, as the child uses the imagination to expand the world. For example, many toys are not played with as the manufacturer intended, so that the imagination is developed still further. The crayons that are not just used for drawing but also become the vegetables being cooked in a pot and given to teddy to eat, illustrate this very process of continuing imagination.

Figure 2.1 Harry and George empty the store cupboard and create their 'house'

The child is readily playing 'as if' as the dramatic imagination develops, and the limits imposed are usually those from adults, as mothers will say:

'No that's not to eat, that's for drawing' or 'That's not a car that's your spoon.'

It would seem that mothers and many adults have a conflict between allowing the imagination of the child and imposing logical facts. The child rapidly discovers when it is appropriate for the imagination and when everyday reality is necessary. Problems only start when there are extremes and children play *only* in their imagination or else respond *only* in logical factual ways.

As the child plays more and more with things beyond the body, we can see the emergence of the stage of *projection* (P) or *projective play*. As the child moves beyond the immediate sensory experience of toys, more complicated scenarios begin to emerge, cat feels poorly, clown is hungry, the dolls' house is used to tell a story, teddy and rabbit go to the seaside. Stories and music are important in the projective enactment of short scenes. The child is increasingly able to play with other children and group scenes with two or three children are devised, often with an adult as arbiter. Although the child uses different voices for the puppets and the dolls it is still termed projective play rather than dramatic play. Projective play includes all types of drawing and crayoning, telling stories about the picture, modelling and clay work, jigsaws, the farm yard and so on. In projective play the child is creating the world outside of him or herself and using a variety of media to do that.

Probably the telling of a story with characters and voices is the nearest projective activity to the next stage, that of *role* (R), *dramatic play* and the creating of characters. We can observe role activity very early in a child's development as they mimic different voices, put on dressing-up clothes, or say in a deep voice, 'I'm the monster – are you frightened?' These are usually brief moments of role activity rather than the sustaining of a role and a scene; much of the role activity is linked with sensory experience and the emotions of fear and pleasure. Dramatic convention is also used in storytelling by children of three years old, but it is usually projective activity rather than a dramatized event. The projective story is told in various voices and through different objects. However, once the role stage is reached, there is much less use of projective objects. The main props are dressing up clothes and stuff to create a scene – a house or a cave and so on.

Rather than the telling of a story, either by an adult or the child, children now start to dramatize the stories, take on roles and play out various characters, rather then doing this through the materials and media. Children are very happy to take on several roles in the enactment of a story, rather than our adult convention of playing just one part!

Children are also constantly clarifying people's roles and relationships, and will keep asking them their name and what they do, even though they have asked the same question three minutes before. 'What's your name?' 'Where are you going?' 'Why?' 'Where are you going?' 'What for?'

Are you my friend? You are my friend but you are not my best friend. You are a my friend and I am your friend too. Are you Mummy's friend? And Daddy's? But you are my friend aren't you?

Figure 2.2 Sophie's card

Figure 2.3 Mummy and the baby in her tummy by Harry

Grandma: Once upon a time there was a little boy who went shopping...

Harry: ...and found a big poo...

Grandma: He was looking for a present for Daddy for his birthday...

Harry: ...and bought a big poo...

Grandma: Harry, I'm bored...

Harry: (*after a thoughtful pause*) No you're not, you're Grandma.

✢   ✢   ✢

Child: I do love Grandpa, I want to marry him when I'm big.

Mother: You can't marry Grandpa,

Child: Why can't I?

Mother: Because he's my father.

Child: Well you married my father.

Children will say, 'Let's play at being children', or will say to a mother, 'Let's pretend that you are my Mummy'. Children, it seems, have no problems about the crossing over of these realities. They are now moving forward into the new stage of dramatic playing, and the more varied the earlier stages of embodiment and projection, the greater the range of exploration of roles and scenes in this stage. Just as during earlier playing stages children would repeat various playing they found enjoyable, whether action or stories or sensation, similarly children will also repeat dramatic scenes that they enjoy, sometimes transposing the events into different characters. Children will re-invent, write new endings, turn humour into tragedy and make a comic farce of a serious tale. They experiment with the structure of stories and plays, the rhythms of narrative and the play and rhyming of words, and the difference between pretending and reality.

> Once upon a time, three ladies went into the wood. Then the old lady died and they went home and had tea.

✛   ✛   ✛

Harry: Grandma, let's play seaside again.

Grandma: Who is going to the seaside today?

Harry: Postman Pat, Buzz, Esmeralda, the dog...

Grandma: Are we taking a picnic?

Harry: Yes – fish fingers, juice, chips, and wine.

Then follows an elaborate game with cars, toys, an ambulance going to the seaside with all the characters; various rescues take place; a car gets stuck in the sand, a person starts to drown in the sea. The characters light a fire, cook their tea and then there is a thunder storm. Everyone gets soaking wet so they

Figure 2.4 Harry, 3, teaching George, 18 months, how to be Batman

dry out by the fire before packing up to go home. This is the repetitive story that has to be played every time I visit and visitors who don't know the story have to be taught it. Notice how it gets amalgamated when Harry has to share his drama with Sophie.

Sophie: Let's play princesses.

Harry: I want to play seaside.

Grandma: Let's all go on a boat.

Harry: And catch sharks.

Sophie: I'm going to be the cat on the boat.

An adventure story enfolds with people falling overboard and being rescued and sharks being caught and cooked for dinner. A big storm comes and rocks the boat and then the boat sails home again. Harry and Sophie slip in and out of different roles: first someone who falls in the water and is chased by a shark; then being the shark and chasing the people; then being the cook and chopping up the shark to eat as shark soup.

> Stephen: I don't want you at my house – go home to your house.

> Aunt: (*goes out of the door and comes back*) I've been to my house and now I've come back to your house.

> Stephen: No! Not pretend – really go to your own house – you're not my friend today.

The three stages of embodiment – projection – and role (EPR) are crucial for human development and cannot be replaced by other types of playing such as technological play. During these three stages, not only is an understanding of everyday reality and the imagination being developed but the child's understanding of 'selfhood' and 'otherhood' is being established. This understanding of course is influenced by the values of the society, and is shaped by culture. Children are learning the norms and values of their own social group as well as the limits being imposed on their behaviour, in other words there is no such thing as 'free playing' or 'free drama' as limits will always be placed – usually by an arbitrating adult. Playing is also contained in another way; it is often contained by the *convention* of the scene or drama being played out. Children will say, 'Mummies don't talk like that', 'we don't eat cake for breakfast', and 'babies can't drive cars', often in an echo of the voices of the adults around them but also from their own limits in terms of their imagination. Monsters can turn into quite conventional creatures, 'the really scary monster got tired so he had a glass of milk and went to sleep'.

The EPR is the bedrock of children's development into adulthood – it is not their psychological or physical or emotional development – it is their *dramatic development* – from which all other development emerges. The dramatic development that enables the body self and other, the projective self and other and the role self and other to become established, means that it influences all physical and mental life and relationships. I am unable to relate to other people unless I have developed my own 'self and other identity'. EPR means identity and identity means a social construct more than a psychological one.

Furthermore, during the EPR development, the child is gradually learning about reality and the imagination. The child assimilates experiences from the world around – 'it's hot' or 'it's noisy' or 'I feel tired' on the one hand, and is able to imagine the exact opposite on the other. In 'let's pretend',

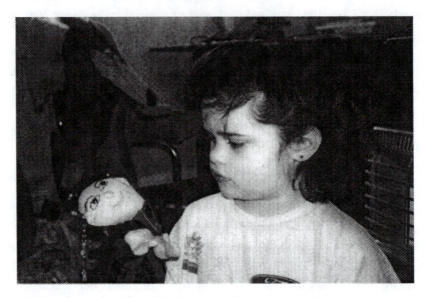

Figure 2.5 Sophie, age six, role playing stories with a hand puppet

the child is entering the world of the imagination, or dramatic reality, and is expressing or creating events that are at variance with the actual world. As we said above, some children are not allowed to develop their imagination and others live completely in their let's pretend world. What is needed is a balance between the two and the capacity to move in and out of the everyday world and the imagined world.

Since we recall and recount our tales in dramatic form, whether we are telling an event to a friend or going over it in our own heads, we need to elaborate the dramatic skills necessary for this communication. We construe the world in dramatic form and we hold dramatic discourse. The foundations of this are laid in childhood after our predisposition towards dramatic organization which started *in utero*.

However, if these foundations have not been laid it is not irretrievable, since the potential has been there from birth but has not been developed. This is where dramatherapy and some forms of theatre-in-education come into their own. The potential is always there and a sensitive dramatherapist or sometimes a theatre practitioner will be able to assist children and adults redress the balance.

Exercises

The following questions will help you recall the earlier stages of your own dramatic history. You may need assistance from other family members to fill in the gaps, and there may be family photographs that can also help you.

Childhood (4–7 years)

You may need to spend a few moments recalling any special landmarks, especially as our memory can get hazier the further we go back; perhaps there were some significant spaces, hidey holes, clothes and so on that may help you recreate this earlier time in your life.

1. Describe any playground games that you used to enjoy playing and mention those that you did not enjoy but maybe were expected to play.

2. Write down any stories that you like to hear over and over again and whether you enjoyed enacting these stories. What character did you imagine yourself to be while listening or enacting?

3. Describe any imaginary friends you had and the sorts of conversations you would have with each other. Did you have adventures together? Any other activities you would do together?

4. Describe (or draw) any special toys that were like your personal friends or companions. Did they have names? What scenes would you play out together?

5. Were the 'dramas' you enacted private dramas? Were you ever stopped by an adult from playing these scenes?

6. Describe your favourite play activities at this age and whether you played with others or on your own. Did you have special scenes that you enjoyed repeating? Special rhymes that you liked to hear again?

7. When did adults or older children join in play and games with you and when did you play with other young children or on your own?

8. Can you recall adults playing parts in the dramas with you or were they the story teller or did you 'perform' for them?

9. Did you experience childhood fears of any kind? For example recurring nightmares? Monsters under the bed? Spooky sounds in the cistern?

10. Did you have a magic place that you went to in your imagination, or a special place where you could hide and imagine it to be somewhere magic?

You have already done a lot of writing and recording; maybe you need some breaks and to continue this later. Again, leave time to do some processing with your co-dramatist, your group, or your internal guide.

Infancy (0–3 years)

This next stage will be to see what you can remember from even earlier in your life, or to find others to help prompt you. Record any memories however fleeting, especially any sensations: that is, taste, smell, touch, sight and hearing.

11. Do you recall any special toy or possession? Did it have a name? Describe and draw what you can remember.

12. Do you remember talking to this special toy and answering *as if* you were the toy?

13. What sensory experience can you recall about this toy? (smell, taste, sound, touch, sight).

14. Can you recall any singing games at this time?

15. Can you recall any stories or rhymes?

16. Do you remember drawing or painting or crayoning?

17. Do you remember playing with clay or similar substance? What did it feel like and what did you make?

18. Describe any other toys or sets of toys that you played with at this time. Did you tell stories with them?

19. Do you remember anything about the clothes you wore? Colours? Texture? Smell?

20. What can you remember about food? Favourite food? Its texture?

21. Can you recall anything about water such as playing or bathtime?

22. What physical movements can you remember such as rocking or clapping?

23. What physical movements can you remember that were shared with an adult? Who usually instigated the movements?

24. Can you recall adults selecting toys and activities on your behalf?

25. Can you recall adults censoring any of your playing activities?

Discuss your answers with your guide or group. Do you recall having roles or qualities ascribed to you by adults? 'She was always a shy child'. 'John, why are you always clumsy?'. Can you remember general experiences of creating houses or nesting spaces or places where something magic could happen? Draw them or make a note of them as part of your own development.

CHAPTER THREE

Processing Your Own Dramatized History
'Untangling the thread'

This chapter is concerned with looking at drama from our own experience. It may be that your immediate thoughts about the words 'drama' and 'theatre' are larger than life experiences that we see reported in the press such as 'Hi-jack drama', 'theatre of war', 'no end in sight for siege drama'. If we say to someone 'don't be so theatrical' we usually mean that they are going 'over-the-top' (also a war phrase) in terms of extreme behaviour. Theatrical language is used in reportage and everyday discourse to highlight events that are larger than life.

However, they tend to be in such common use that they do not make the same impact; and I am still wondering about a recent statement that this war was going to be 'the mother of all wars'. Perhaps the reader made some connections when I described mothers as the primary instigators of dramas. However, let us stay with our current thoughts and experiences of drama and theatre.

Our own experience is a primary means of understanding and learning throughout our lives. When we do things and discover through that doing, the learning usually stays with us. We can all remember as children experiencing pain when we touched lighted matches or the stove; we had to do it for ourselves no matter how often we were told not to touch – it's hot! In terms of our own experience we learn things through our own bodies before we learn in other ways. We learn from the way we are held or not held; we learn through our five senses; we learn through hot and cold and shades of temperature; and we learn about bodies together and bodies apart – not only human bodies but the bodies of our pets and toys. We do not learn in isolation but in relation to the reaction and response from others.

You may now wish to record some impressions here and now in your notebook before we start to explore further. Write down any impressions, thoughts, images and so on that occur to you right now, whether or not you have written down any responses to earlier questions in the book.

If you decide not to write anything down, nevertheless you will have had some memories and reactions to the questions, just from reading them through. Before you are tempted to attach psychological 'meaning' to these memories, read the next section which suggests a different 'frame' or 'stage' within which we may experience or view or understand your history.

It is most important to know that the task of this chapter is not to start analyzing bits and pieces and playing the psychotherapist; indeed that would be counter-productive: it could well interrupt the creative process in which we are engaged. It would be changing the goal-posts and making use of different theoretical constructs, rather than making use of the drama itself.

We shall need to be constantly on our guard since psychotherapy is embedded in our thinking, and indeed in popular language such as: 'that was a Freudian slip' or 'his ego is very inflated' or 'what are you avoiding?'. It takes an act of will to stay in a different mind set, or even allow us to think that there are alternatives; in this instance we are staying within the dramatic framework even though we may want to side-step.

For example, in a recent discussion that I was leading on the several artistic therapies, a situation emerged in which we debated the differences between: the arts therapies considered as forms of psychotherapy, and arts therapies which emphasized the healing potential of the art form itself. The former group discussed the primacy of the relationship between client and therapist as being the foundation of the therapy. The latter group maintained that it was the relationship between the client and the art form that was the basis of the therapy. In one, the relationship between client and therapist is facilitated by the art; in the other, the therapist facilitates the relationship with the art form. We then realized that we had discovered a major difference between the various approaches to artistic therapies. This one is a very important difference in philosophy and indeed in belief, concerning the therapeutic outcomes of artistic experience. I will discuss these issues more fully when we talk further about dramatherapy theory and application.

Meanwhile, I just want to state that I do not wish us to come to a full stop at the moment, which would be the result of analyzing the material; a comma or semi-colon is sufficient for us to pause. If we undertake something creative and then stop to analyze it, we actually bring the process to a halt. Once a creative process is engendered, it continues to spiral even when we are not actively engaged with it. I do not say that it continues to work in the unconscious because I have my own doubts that there is such an entity as '*the* unconscious' : a big black pit of unacceptable thoughts and feelings.

As an alternative, let us consider our life to be one enormous theatre with various episodes and roles and events packed away as 'past productions'. Other events continue throughout our lives in new versions or rewrites. Some perhaps have been discarded because we did not understand them, or a tragedy was ignored when it seemed too painful and unresolved. We are going to use a theatre as a means of processing our own experience and see where it might lead us. First of all, let us remind ourselves of the variations and complexities that make up a building that we call a theatre and the contents that are both visible and invisible, and accessible and inaccessible. Then we shall consider the various people involved in the functioning of a theatre, who may well help us structure our own roles and characters as well as those of others in our life dramas. As you read the following description of a theatre, be aware of any images that are familiar or that grab your attention or that have no connection to yourself at all. Some key words have been highlighted, but you may well find other key words of your own. Remember too, that a theatre is often referred to as *the house.* So we talk about the 'house being full', we refer to staff being 'front of house'.

First we must consider the structure of the theatre itself. Is it **fixed** in terms of the seating and the stage? A fixed space means that we can only direct certain types of play, whereas a theatre that can have its seating rearranged lends itself to a wider range of plays. Similarly the stage itself can have pieces added onto it (the singer Al Jolson insisted on having a ramp running down the centre of the audience so that he could have more contact); stages can be rebuilt at different heights and different levels as well as different shapes. The seating and the stage can both be **flexible** within certain limits. It can be in the round or in a rectangle.

What about the lighting of this theatre? In a conventional play, the audience lights are **dimmed** and the stage is **illuminated**, and modern theatre technology means that the stage lighting can be very **complex** and **subtle**, with some areas illuminated and some dimmed; a rainbow of colours and special effects such as strobes and thunder flashes (Jolson insisted on keeping the lights on in the auditorium so that he could see the faces of the audience). This is all very different from the row of candles at the front of the stage in the pre-electricity days, or the use of natural daylight when theatres were open to the skies. Are the lighting effects in your personal theatre very sudden in their changes or do we find a gradual change or melange? How is the lighting controlled? As well as the lighting of course, there will be some kind of **sound system**, which may be a tape recorder with speakers in the auditorium for the playing of music and sound effects. There will also be various devices for creating certain sounds such as thunder sheets, rain sieves, bells and chimes; unless these of course have been pre-recorded. Often there is a **lighting and sound box**, which is usually situated at the back of the auditorium from where light and sound can be operated.

What about the scenery and curtains? The space may simply have black 'drapes' that adapt for any production and on which lights are successfully projected. There may be 'flats', the one dimensional pieces of scenery that are painted to represent different scenes: indoors or outdoors, olden times or modern times, simple or exotic; the flats become **three dimensional** when illuminated by the lights and the whole scene is physically transformed in a convincing way. We know that they are pieces of canvas painted in the scene department, but we are usually willing to **suspend our disbelief** for the duration of the play.

There may also be **curtains** that **divide** the audience from the actors at the beginning and the end; the curtain may slowly drop from above or a pair of curtains may close. The back of the stage may have a **backdrop**, where a scene or symbol is painted, against which the play is being enacted. And of course we must not forget the moveable scenery such as furniture, trees, park benches and the like. It is always interesting to ask the question, when is something a piece of scenery and when is it an actors' prop!

Then of course there is the scenery that comes down from above; scenery that is **flown in** can only exist in a theatre space that has enough height. Then curtains, large flats and portable scenery of all kinds can be dropped in at the appropriate moment. And of course the **safety curtain** must be shown to the audience at some point during the show.

Is there a space under the stage? Maybe it is for storage or it can function as a part of the performance space. There may be trap doors, steps down below; it may be used to add two levels to the stage; things may descend or emerge.

Within this space there are also exits and entrances. Usually these are on either side of the stage, otherwise known as the **wings**. One of my early books on dramatherapy had a subtitle **Waiting in the Wings** (*Dramatherapy with Families Groups and Individuals*), and some time after the book was published I dreamed that I was actually waiting in the wings of a theatre, together with one of the actors in the company. I remarked that his black T shirt was short sleeved, unlike my own, so he might be seen. It was indeed some years later before I was once more seen on stage!

The exits and entrances may be few or many and can vary from a single space for both getting on and off the stage to several on either side, through the back of the stage, up through the trap door or through the audience. They may be open and grand or narrow and difficult; however we may describe these exits and entrances they are the point of transition for being **on stage**, and are therefore of crucial importance both to our theatre of life, as well as the theatre itself.

So far we have addressed the immediate spaces themselves but there are yet more that are necessary for a play to function. Either at the sides of the stage or underneath it or above it there are **dressing rooms** or tiring rooms. These are rooms for the transitions from the everyday roles to our stage characters, which have mirrors and bright lights. Small theatres may only have the smallest of token space compared with the lavish suites of our more splendid theatre. Most dressing rooms are somewhere in between these two extremes, and unless you are a big star, they are shared. They should have washbasin and loo facilities nearby but sometimes studio theatres are built that have the amenities in another building! Not very helpful when one is supposed to drink large amounts of water to moisten one's vocal cords! There are hooks and wardrobe rails for costumes, and tables for make-up and hair pieces. Small props may be in the dressing room or on tables at the side of the stage, in the wings.

Behind the scenes – more spaces. Since I suggested we use the image of a large theatre, there are therefore other spaces in this building: places where **scenery and props** are constructed and painted; **the wardrobe** department where costumes are made and maintained, with washing and sewing machines ; a **rehearsal studio** with some minimal furniture and gaffer tape on the floor, marking out certain spaces. In a small number of theatres there is a voice department with a voice room and possibly a movement department which may well use the rehearsal room. There is also **storage space** with racks of costumes, hampers of accessories and props, shelves of masks and wigs on stands, and flats and curtains. All of this stuff may be recycled and used again.

The foyer and box office spaces. This is where the audience begin their journey into the theatre when they purchase their **tickets** at the box office or meet with friends or have a drink in the bar or a meal in the cafe. There are places to leave your coats and bags and loos and wash basins. There are also offices for the administration of the theatre which are separate from the spaces for the general public.

Outside the theatre there is a car park and gardens and a walkway to the street. Outside the theatre are the several entrances and exits which each have different functions. There is the **public entrance** for the audience, the **stage door** for the actors and theatre workers, and large doors for the removal of scenery; these doorway are separated without compromise. There are also additional exits which are permanently labelled, like in an aircraft, which are fire exits. **Safety** is paramount in an environment that is literally, as well as metaphorically **inflammable.**

This is a very broad and brief description of a typical large theatre space and the functions for which these spaces are divided. Let us now consider the people that work in these spaces, as we continue to consider a theatre as a model or perhaps a metaphor for our dramatized history.

If we look at a theatre programme, most of the people involved in a production will be listed in their categories. The performers, directing and stage management staff will also have their biographies. People are grouped according to their function and those who are most **visible** are the **performers** who usually consist of actors and actresses, dancers, singers, musicians (though musicians in a play are sometimes concealed partially or totally). Those who are **less visible** are the **stage management** and the stage crew, unless the latter need to come on stage to move scenery between scenes or acts. The stage management see that the show happens. They oversee all the practical things, most of which centre around time and time management.

Before a production can be seen by the public there is a coming together of the **director** together with the performers, designers and the administrators; they do not usually all group together in one place but there are many meeting as the director consults with the administration, especially finance; the design team for suggestions for staging, costumes, lighting and effects. As the rehearsals progress designs are created in miniature with samples of material and colour schemes. The rehearsals of course cannot start until the actors have been auditioned, stars invited, contracts agreed and a company assembled. The director will have already had some thoughts about the play and will usually begin the rehearsal period with a read through of the text. Publicity is already being planned in order to profile the play through the media, posters and mailing lists. As the weeks progress a more definitive rehearsal period is structured, costumes are being fitted, and the point named at which the actors must be **off the book**. From now on the director will use a **prompter** for when the actors forget their lines. It may be the stage manager during the rehearsal period, but is usually a professional prompter once the play has opened, though some theatres have dispensed with the prompter's role. The rehearsals end with a call for the press photographers, technical rehearsals, and one or more dress rehearsals. Sometimes the show opens with several previews and then a Press Night, after which the play is up and running, either with a fixed run, or in repertory with other plays or a fixed run with the possibility of continuing if the play is a success, Of course there are plays that have been so badly received that they close after a few days; there are also plays that have been slammed by the press that the public have enjoyed. There are many variations of this theme and we have already introduced another category of people involved and that is the press – both the **photographers** and the **theatre critics**. The press have a transitory relationship with a play, and good quotes are used for further publicity.

The front of house staff are selling tickets, taking bookings before the play opens. Once it is due to open, the increased staff manage the front of house so that everything proceeds smoothly. You cannot enter the auditorium unless you have a ticket, and there is someone on guard to check your ticket as well as bar your way until the appropriate time. There are more staff inside who will sell you your programme and show you to your seat.

Almost always on time, the lights dim, the staff melt away and the play begins.

We have now considered the wider context of our theatre rather than just thinking in terms of the audience and the actors. We have thought about the spaces that are not seen and the people who are invisible in a performance. The people who are most visible, the performers, are those who are least accessible. People may wait at the stage door to ask for autographs or will try to gain access to the backstage area through ruses.

As the audience gradually becomes involved both as a collective and as individuals we react to what the actors present to us. We may know the play or it might be a complete surprise; we may be attending because of what the critics have said or because we are joining friends on a social occasion or because we are doing research into a text. Usually we stay for the duration of the play, though there will be times when we leave at the interval. However, it is interesting to note that we can never leave the theatre in a hurry. Just as it takes time to get into the theatre, and if we are late, we may not be allowed in, it also takes time to leave. The beginning and the end of the performance is ritualized in familiar ways, to provide the transitions between the outside world and the world of the theatre.

This detailed description of the theatre structure and the various roles that are necessary for it to function, begins to expand our awareness of what a theatre actually is and what it does. Many people only consider the actual play that they go to see and the actors that are involved. The complexities of actually getting a 'show on the road' are not often addressed. The major organization and co-ordination, however modest the production, takes a wide range of complementary skills. Also the time factor – from the moment the ideas for the production are proposed to when it is actually made public to an audience, takes several months; even longer if a new play is being commissioned. So the creative process that goes on before a play is made visible is where much of the struggle and exploration goes on. Being in a play is one of the greatest social skills exercises of all time because in the end, there has to be co-operation in order for the production to happen, and there has to be awareness of the skills and necessity of other people and their roles. Theatre people develop a camaraderie between themselves which could be compared to an extended family, and certainly theatre people look after their own when there is an accident, illness or old age.

Immediately we become aware of the larger process as I have described above, our perception begins to expand to take in this new world. The detailed interweaving of text, design and performance can be seen as a highly specialized form of structured creativity. It is because of this expansion of perception that I suggest dramatherapy's unique function is to assist us grow larger, metaphorically speaking. The theatre process enables us to go beyond ourselves, to transform our experience from the mundane to the metaphysical.

Thus the EPR described earlier in relation to our childhood dramatic development, expands to being larger than life when it becomes a Theatre of Health and Healing. When people in dramatherapy groups are able to make their experience physical and make it larger than life; when they can create enormous masks and effigies; when they can take on mythic roles and characters, we can see that their EPR becomes extended in movement, voice, objects, space, themes and roles. It enables them to transform their experience and go beyond themselves. A metaphysical experience to expand our perceptions of ourselves and the world.

In order to do this it is necessary to have a perception of what the theatre actually is in form and structure and the devices that we can call upon to enable the process of creation. Theatre visits both to see productions as well as behind the scenes are an important stimulus to people's creative development. The initial shock at seeing this glorious sunset reduced to a piece of canvas daubed with paint, the golden shields constructed from hammered bottle tops, and the harsh landscape created from polystyrene, brings home to us the two realities. The everyday and the dramatic, the mundane and the imaginative.

Many clients respond to the idea of dramatherapy by saying 'I can't act' or 'I'm too shy to stand up in front of people'. Dramatherapists should create a wider understanding of theatre processes so that people can find their own strengths within that. The challenge of transforming some rubbish into a magical forest or finding exactly the right sound for a given effect is all part of the process of the creation of theatre. It encourages resourcefulness as well as creativity as the non-existent budget has to clothe and stage the project or play. And the biggest challenge of all is, will it 'work'? Will the production as a whole work, will the timing work, will the effects work, will the interpretation work... None of these things will be known until this piece is actually before an audience who, by and large, will let the company know whether they think it works. The culmination of our dramatic development in one form or another is to present something to a witnessing public; and it is the relationship between the performers and the public that creates the experience that we call theatre. This live experience cannot be replaced by any technology or virtual reality; it has to exist in the theatrical moment, perhaps a split second that is crucial out of all the months of preparation. As witnesses to theatre performances it is rare that we hold the production as a whole in our minds unless we have seen it before or know the play very well. What usually happens is that we recall special moments or happenings within the play as a whole where we were transported somewhere special. It is those moments that we usually share with other people in the 'do you recall when...' communication of post show discussion.

I have attempted to place our experience within the theatre as a whole, to enable us to see it as something larger than ourselves and as something that can enlarge and transform our experiences. By using the wider structure of theatre as a whole our dramatherapy groups can be a part of this process and journey to a place where they have not journeyed before.

This progression can be the same for the audience and for the performer and can be a way of structuring our dramatherapy and therapeutic theatre. This process needs more time that the conventional therapeutic hour or hour and a half, which is why most of my work needs three or so hours. Words like awakening, challenge, surprise, revolution, revelation and strength, occur to me as I write this description of theatre. They are all words that have a place in a dramatherapy storehouse.

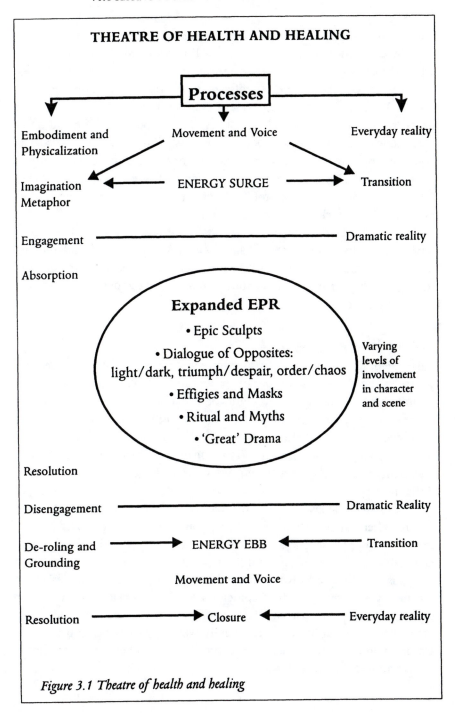

Figure 3.1 Theatre of health and healing

Exercises

Earlier on I suggested that you wrote down words associated with your experience of theatre. Please add to this list any words from this chapter, whether from areas of theatre space or from roles and functions of the people who work there, that seemed significant as you read the description of the theatre. You may find there are phrases which occur to you that link with your dramatized history, such as 'I was always in the spotlight', 'I could never remember my lines', 'I never took off my mask'. You will start to associate scenes in your life with being the performer or the director or the prompter or the audience. What is the first recollection that you have of being able to influence the design of your life? Think about dramas that have been packed away and not recycled in your present life.

You now have some practical tasks to take this process a step further. They will both require larger pieces of paper (at least A3 size), pencils, crayons and felt pens. If you do not wish to do this exercise, just mark it as you read through with your own recollections. You may think about how you could apply it with your clients.

Exercise 1: Ground plan of a theatre

Take one of the large pieces of paper and draw a ground plan of a theatre for yourself. The above descriptions of spaces can act as a prompter, so you can create a ground plan that feels right for you and your dramatized history. Some space may be bigger than others so you might have a small stage and a very big storage area, or the boundaries between the different areas may be less defined than in most theatres. Try not to be too logical but use the theatre metaphor as a way of structuring your memories of your past life in a different way.

Note down dramas from your life that you feel were more important than others. Where are these located in your ground plan – the rehearsal room? At the stage door? Use crayons to colour significant areas including those affected by the mood of different lights. At the moment we are considering your past dramatized history, not your current life. On the ground plan, do the areas you have highlighted coincide with the observations you made in the questionnaire, in terms of clusters and patterns? There are no idealized pictures that are 'right', there are merely ways of experiencing things and alerting you to potential change and choice through new understanding – understanding through theatre.

Exercise 2: Roles and functions

On a second piece of paper, look at the various roles that belong to the spaces that you have now drawn. The question is, who functioned in your past theatre and what did they do? During our early life there will be a series of roles that are taken on by others and some might be combined. For example we may feel that our parents shared the directing and stage management between them and it was Grandma who was the financial administrator. Draw a series of circles around a central circle that represents you and **write down their function in relation to a theatre role**. You can also indicate the relationship between these roles, whether they changed, and how skilled people were in them. You may want to indicate more about these roles through the use of colour. Try to keep it within the metaphor of theatre.

Exercise 3: Your own theatre roles

In the above diagram you drew a circle to represent yourself in the middle of the other circles which represented others. Now take another piece of paper and draw a larger circle. You are still going to focus on your past dramas but now to concentrate on the various roles that you yourself played. You could represent these by drawing circles within the big circle. Try not to draw any roles in isolation but in relation to the spaces that you created on your ground plan. Again the roles can be coloured and give some indication of those roles that dominate more strongly than others. Did you duplicate or imitate roles that were also taken by people around you? Were there ones that were more successful than others? As you progressed through your life until now, did any of the roles change substantially? Are there roles that you wish you could change or modify or just give up? Do you want to maintain the wardrobe of others for the rest of your life?

You now have three pieces of paper which together illustrate your own theatre history on a ground plan and on two role plans. Place them side by side and consider yourself in the total context of what you have recorded. Be aware of the various colours on the different sheets and the progression through to adulthood.

What play is being enacted out in this theatre? From all the various smaller dramas that you have recorded, what is the bigger story that took place. What is its title? It may be one you make up or the title of an existing play or novel or film.

Is this same drama continuing or are the changes that you hoped would happen now falling into place?

Finally, what play or what story does your life remind you of? A Shakespeare Comedy? A Greek Tragedy? A Contemporary Political Play? Find time to re-read the play or story or ideally see the play and reflect again on what you have written down.

Later on, take your own life-theatre into a bigger theme, and make it a part of the great story. Perhaps the big story will give you new possibilities and choices. You may have pictures and images and poems that will elaborate your story.

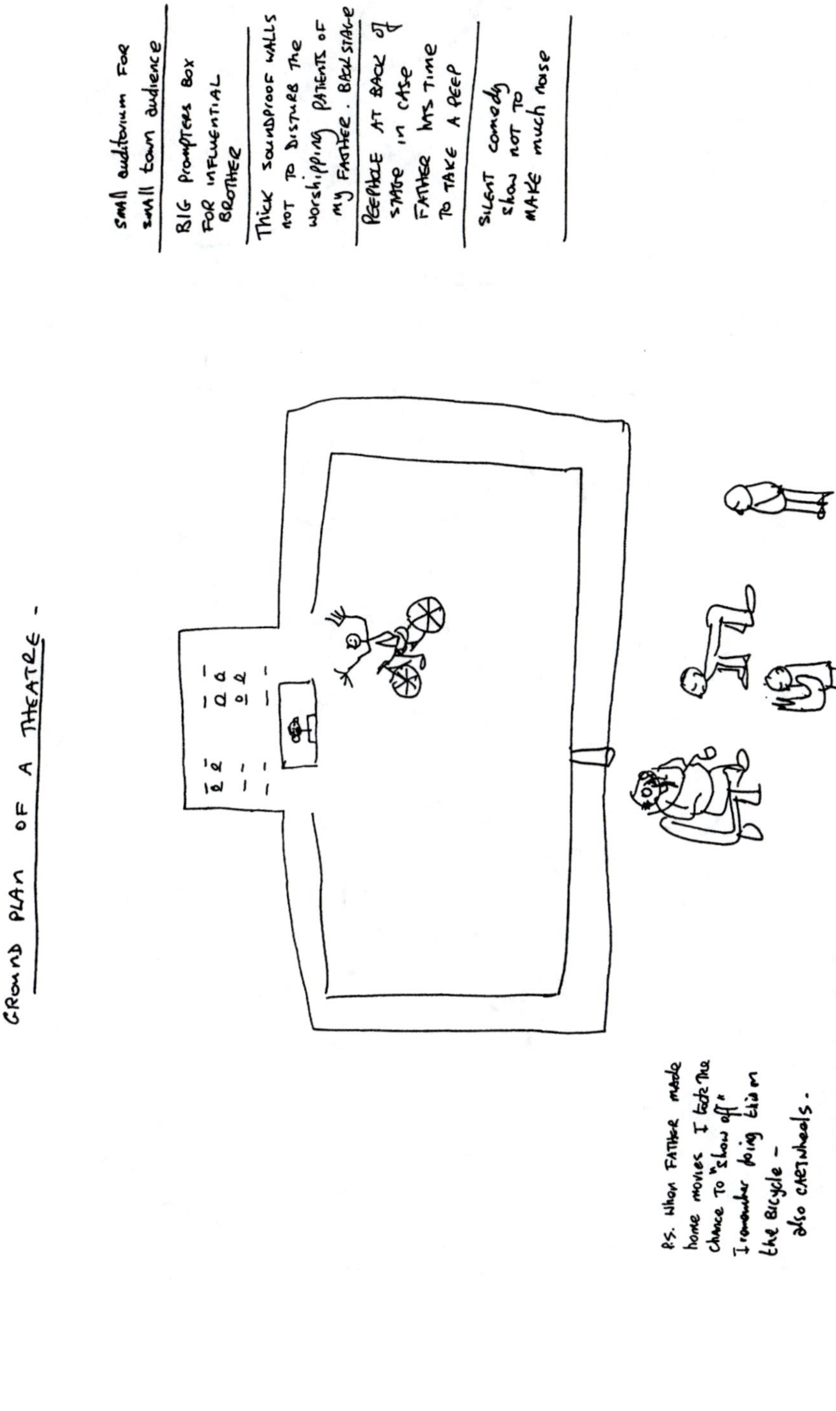

GROUND PLAN OF A THEATRE -

small auditorium for small town audience

BIG prompters box for influential brother

Thick soundproof walls not to disturb the worshipping parents of my father. Bad stage

Peephole at back of stage in case father has time to take a peep

Silent comedy show not to make much noise

P.S. When father made home movies I took the chance to "show off" I remember being thrown the bicycle - also cartwheels.

Figure 3.2 Sample ground plan of a theatre

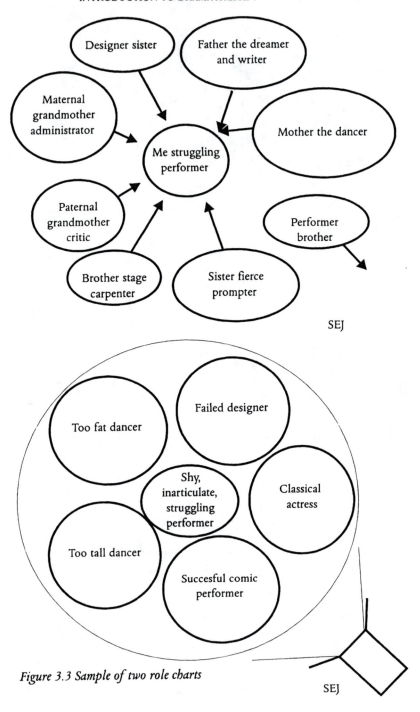

Figure 3.3 Sample of two role charts

CHAPTER FOUR

Transitional Dramas
'Holding onto the thread'

This chapter continues to consider the observable dramas that take place in our lives, and the relationship that these dramas have to the people around us. We will also see how the dramatic imagination continues to develop, and slowly separates from the reality of the everyday world.

We have considered the dramas that take place in the first seven years of life and saw how embedded the dramatic experience is in both parents and infants, and how the child's dramatic imagination starts to develop before it can even walk, initially through the imagination of the mother. We now look at how the dramatic imagination and the drama become part of the process that separates us from dependency. It also enables the development of individual identity, as well as being a means of bonding us to our peers instead of our parents. The process continues as we mature through the peer group into adult life and the cycle is completed when we then make choices concerning partners and parenthood.

In dramatic playing, children find resolutions, challenge reality, invent worlds and develop their imagination, but it is achieved within the protected world of adults. Indeed adults, especially parents, are very much involved in the drama: on the one hand they, especially mothers, have helped to foster the primary dramatic act and the dramatic imagination, and on the other hand they take on the role of arbiter in the play and games of young children. The child is also beginning to distinguish between the reality of everyday experience and the reality of the dramatic imagination. This concept of the two realities will be explored more fully.

The child begins to take examples of behaviour of all kinds from the parents, in other words, begins the process of role-modelling. We shall now see not only how this develops much more strongly as children grow older but also how choices are then made about accepting or rejecting the roles of the parents and other significant adults. This again can be cyclic as often the period of teen time is the period of rejection of parental roles, only for them to be rediscovered as young adults. We appear to dramatize a closeness and distance in relation to our peers and parents which are ritualized in statements about sameness and difference. These similarities and distances can be very volatile in young people and high drama can be enacted in families with such ferocity that sometimes the parental bonds can be severed and the child leaves home or, in extreme situations, taken into care with alternative families.

I want to explore the extent to which these dramas need to be made explicitly symbolic without their spilling over into actual experience. How much is it possible to ritualize rebellion rather than to have actual rebellion? My belief is that the ritual can make the rebellious statement accompanied by strong feelings, but difficulties arise if the statement is taken as a literal statement rather than a ritualized and symbolic one. Life seems to be a continuous process of sorting out these two realities, with a child saying, 'I didn't mean it, I was only pretending' or a teenager saying 'I wasn't going to actually hit him, I was just being threatening'.

From about the age of seven we can observe that the drama of children shifts from dramatic playing involving embodiment – projection – role (EPR), to a greater understanding of the dramatic processes which are still very physical and the idea of constructing a drama. Older children have a stronger idea of narrative and a clarity of roles, something happens and there is a resolution. Children between the ages of seven and eleven readily create their own dramas in their peer groups as well as responding to drama as a subject in school or in a drama club. Often their plays are based on TV stories, soaps, hospitals or specific heroes and heroines.

They also dramatize their views and experiences about families, which may reflect their own experience in a family or it may be the creation of an idealized family; we may even find a dramatization of someone's fears about a family. It is less usual at this age for children to dramatize issues from the wider world, or the debate of social issues; however there may well be *dramas of care* as a hero or heroine saves the world from destruction, rescues people from a fire, performs a life saving operation and so on. Moral issues and social responsibility are very often enacted in stereotyped forms, as well as the usual cowboys and Indians, or battles of all kinds. Children seem to gain satisfaction in the work of planning a play, deciding on stories and roles, and ways of achieving their effects. Very intense debate ensues concerning the right way to do something, and leaders emerge as directors.

Two girls were creating their own drama:

Sophie: 'You be the leader and I'll be the master.'

✛   ✛   ✛

Two sisters were planning a play and one said to the other:

'Let's play at being sisters'.

Strong feelings about rightness and justice start to emerge in stories as well as in the everyday world. A colleague was marking some writing about the work of the health visitor, after her visit to a secondary school; she smiled as she read out 'Sometimes the health visitor comes when you have had a heat-attack'; her young son said, 'You shouldn't laugh, they probably couldn't spell sunstroke'.

As children start to approach adolescence the drama can become more self-conscious, and some children stop doing it altogether. They have concerns about being laughed at and are beginning to be aware of their image and bodily changes. The world of secondary school is looming on the horizon and may hold many a terror, and the worlds of home and school seem to have a wider gulf between them. Some junior schools have a policy of children visiting their new school or even spending days there before they actually attend, which is an admirable way of defusing tension.

What has dramatherapy to offer children between the ages of seven years and eleven? Dramatherapy can re-establish the EPR development for those children where it has not occurred or it has become distorted. Dramatic playing emerges and scenes and stories from real life and from the imagination may be enacted, with the proviso that they stay in the reality of the play and are not interpreted. Dramatic play can put the borders in place and create a container for the child within which distressing material can be expressed. Older children also need these forms of dramatherapy and may well play like young children since they have not matured to their age stage. However, one of the goals of the work will be to allow the child to re-establish their dramatic development, and often they will then have the tools to deal with distressing experience, because nightmares, for example, can be contained.

My primary goals in all kinds of therapy are:

- **to re-skill and empower people through the dramatherapy in order for them more ably manage their own lives.**

- **to maximize their dramatic functioning which will bring about the self-healing processes and promote greater well-being.**

I am not interested in 'disclosure work' as such, except when there is a serious illegal offence and prosecution is necessary. Then the disclosure work should not be part of the therapy but be dealt with quite separately. The dramatherapy is for the healing of the experience in cases of trauma, as well as a means of finding coping strengths. In most cases these dramatherapeutic interventions can be quite brief and be based on an honest relationship with a skilled adult who maintains the autonomy and integrity of the child, rather than fostering unhealthy dependency. The child who can play creatively and enact 'self and other' can go a long way towards dealing with life's issues. The development of dramatic strengths enables greater self-healing to take place.

Dramatherapy for young people is about freeing them from imposed malfunction from adults. Inappropriate roles can be placed on them for which they are not equipped.

Other children who have physical damage of any sort also need dramatherapy in order to maximize their dramatic functioning.

Children at this age can also benefit from rehearsal of future events, whether it is a visit to hospital or the start of secondary school. Dramatization of an event that has not yet happened is one of the best ways of gaining mastery over the fear. Just as the enactment of a past nightmare, with the child being able to play the monster rather than the victim, enables the child to take control of the event, the child who can enact something in the future also gains mastery over thoughts and feelings that appear out of control. And of course this reality has to be tested; is the reality of my dramatic imagination going to be born out in the real world when I actually do go to hospital? Again we are sorting out our realities and testing which of our experiences belong in the actual world and which belong to the dramatic imagination.

Young children are constantly sorting their realities and defining what is imaginative and what is for real. As I am writing this piece, Harry, my grandson, comes in and asks me to go shopping in his shop in the garden; I tell him that I must just print one more page and he asks me why. 'So that I will know where I am,' I reply. 'You're in Devonshire Road,' he says immediately. Signposting is something we always need to do and many people who come for therapy have lost their signposts of life, 'I've lost my direction' is often said.

Sorting out realities does not just affect the maturation of children, we seem to continue this sorting throughout our lives. How often do we take umbrage at something someone has said and their rejoinder is 'I was only teasing' or 'it was just a joke'. The other's statement that it was not to be taken seriously does not always assuage the hurt we might feel. Parents and children alike can both recall things that were said or done from early life of which the other has no memory at all:

Mother: 'When you were only ten years old you called me a witch and I've never forgotten it.'

+ + +

Child: (as adult) 'I've never forgiven Dad for forgetting my birthday when he was away. I was twelve.'

+ + +

Parent: 'You never were an easy child to get on with and you've not changed since.'

+ + +

Woman of thirty: 'When I was fourteen my mother said to me, "If you're behaving like that you can find your own home"; so two years later I did and I've not spoken to her since.'

Roles and scenes have become 'fixed' in the perception of the other and they are unable to 'move on', perhaps even for a lifetime. 'Re-working' life experiences is something we seem continually to do. We re-work events that have startled or hurt us, in order to move on. We re-tell the story in different ways to different 'audiences' of friends, neighbours, relatives, police, strangers at a bus stop, long distance family and so on. Usually these audiences give feedback, unlike conventional therapists, so the person telling the event not only receives support and concern, but also different perspectives on the dynamics of the drama.

Friend: 'Are you sure he picked on you deliberately or was your
            work not up to standard that day?'

+   +   +

Mother: 'I am so sorry to hear about the exams. Shall we talk
            about it again tomorrow and see if there is anything that
            can be done?'

If we 'sleep on it', often the situation can change without drastic action or we
wake up in the morning with a solution. Sleep seems to provide us with its
own re-working. Dreams can provide solutions or expositions in dramatic
form.

**Re-working happens when we need to make choices and move
on or when we cannot let go of an event or episode that has disturbed us.**

It is very easy for scenes and roles to become fixed, perceptions distorted and
events taken out of context.

Politicians and other public figures agonise over the fact that what they
say is taken out of context and different meanings placed on their statements.
To illustrate this, the reader will remember a politician making an ironical
statement about young people being employed to gather and export fresh
magic mushrooms. He was pounced upon by the media and accused of
endorsing young people's involvement with drugs. Whereas his *actual*
statement was in the context of the ludicrous law that allows the gathering
and marketing of *any* fresh mushrooms but prohibits these magic mushrooms
once they are dried! His irony was twisted into everyday fact and generated a
whole series of ridiculous dramas.

Perhaps there is some intentionality in this, and that the media and others
deliberately wish to misconstrue what we stay in order to go on creating what
I term 'mischief dramas'. It is a prime example of a statement being taken out
of context and it can be just the same in our memories of roles and situations.
When a young adult says 'You never ever listened to me when I was young';
the unspoken statement may be, 'you never listened to me in the way that I
wanted you to' or 'I didn't want you to listen to me, I wanted to listen to you!'
We have a plethora of 'special moments' that we can recall in our lives that are
usually out of the original context and have a certain gloss put on them, more
often negative than positive.

However, we do not just do this ourselves about our own memories; other people also have specific decontextualized memories about us. For example, someone says to us, 'but you never used to enjoy walking' or 'you always used to like Christmas cake', 'but you always loved going to see musicals'; these statements are taken out of the context in which the original events took place. Not only do we decontextualize them, we may even transpose them from one reality to another and recall something as actual rather than symbolic.

There are also other processes at work here. For example, we may also transpose the realities when we do not have enough information or when a child tries to construe their world through their own limited experience. In my own life, when we were living in an isolated cottage, my paternal grandfather used to send us newspapers and comics through the post each week. As a child of eight, my assumption was that my grandfather must have a newspaper shop and my parents were shocked when they heard me tell this to a friend. 'Wherever did you get that idea? Your grandfather is a businessman,' said my mother. My understanding of reality had to make a substantial shift as well as grasp the subtext that perhaps a newspaper shop was not an appropriate occupation for my grandfather. Of course it took me a while before I realized that a newspaper shop is as good a business as any other!

There is also the question of 'the fixed role'; we sometimes do not like to acknowledge changes in other people and other people will deny changes in us. This is often the case in the 'you always used to...' type of statements. This is especially difficult for young people as they are growing through a series of roles and identities as they move towards adulthood. Part of our transition into adult life is the struggle we experience with various life roles including work, gender, sexual orientation, belief system and culture.

The situation becomes exacerbated in therapy when memories are recounted out of context and in an individual situation; non-interventionist therapists will not usually ask questions to fill out the picture and the only 'other' for the person to explore is the therapist. Frequently, as I have already stated, the therapist does not respond 'as themselves' so no reality is brought into the transaction for the client. Therefore instead of any 're-working' taking place, it is all too often a re-statement and the re-statement may in fact be an inaccurate picture of the actual situation, no matter the feelings being expressed.

In conventional psychotherapy the relationship is the focus of the therapy and it is expected that 'the client' will transfer feelings from the past towards significant others onto the therapist; the 'transference' is the *raison d'être* of psychotherapy. Time, space and regularity, are the control factors in psychotherapy and communication is usually verbal. Psychotherapists say very little unless they make interpretations of the client's material. However, what is not usually acknowledged is that the psychotherapeutic relationship is a dramatic one. The client behaves towards the therapist 'as if' he or she is a significant other; roles are projected onto the therapist who does not enact them. The client will usually assume various roles from their past lives and express them in the therapeutic relationship. Although there are dramatic elements in this relationship, it is not fully understood as a piece of drama and the limits of a dramatization are not understood.

Dramatization needs to be *interactive*, with everyone in acknowledged roles, and the separation of the two realities firmly established. However, although clients are in a partially dramatized scenario, there is no 'getting into role', and no 'de-roling', and there is no transition in or out of the dramatic reality. Clients leave their sessions still in role and have to enter the outside world without transition, often emotional and sometimes confused. The session itself does not acknowledge its basis in drama and the transference is not seen as a variation of 'as if', in other words as a part of dramatic reality.

It is important to contextualize the transference phenomenon and understand it as something that most people do in their ordinary lives and throughout their lives. If you look back at your dramatized history, and give some thought to the times in your life when you needed to re-work an experience, you will find various dramas where you either invented significant others or turned people into someone else, by an act of the dramatic imagination. We continue to familiarise our world by projecting associations from other people onto new people, or by gathering around us people who remind us of our earlier 'significant other'. We all do this and it is a part of our dramatization of life's journey. It only presents difficulties if it gets in the way of our maturation into new roles and relationships, in other words if our role relationships become a *closed role system*.

We want to change jobs, move to a new place, meet someone new or just be different but we find ourselves trapped in our old roles and the scenes that go with them. How often do we struggle to be 'settled cultivators' when we are longing to be 'hunter gatherers'.

If a person has not had enough dramatization in their history, their range of roles and relationships is severely limited and they continue to operate in a closed role system. The person continues to repeat the roles in various guises that have been surrounding him or her from early in their lives. Whereas dramatherapy is able to intervene in this repetitive closed cycle, psychotherapy can reinforce the closed system and repeat the familial patterns of roles.

Dramatherapy enables us to expand our roles in relation to the world and thus our perception of ourselves and others.

I shall discuss role expansion more fully later. Let us return to our role transitions as we move towards adulthood. Role transitions are marked in societies by various rituals or rites, As we move from being a child to being an adolescent, the transition is often marked by changes in expectations, responsibilities, schooling, clothing, life style and so on. The idea is that when a child reaches double figures, childhood is at an end and adolescence begins, although this is often unspoken and does not necessarily apply cross-culturally. For example in some cultures you are a child and then you are an adult; there is not an idea of adolescence. We could view adolescence as a very protracted rite of passage or transition ritual that enables us to change from our child role to our adult one. However, it is a very lengthy one and there is no clear statement of when it has finished. Legally and socially there are different expectations concerning adulthood and if we are students, this continues well into young adult life. Indeed the term 'eternal student' is often a pejorative term, and there is still an ethos of doing 'a proper job of work'; even more interesting when we consider the shortage of jobs that are available.

In western society, although there are various changes that mark the transition from child to adolescent there is not an actual *ritual of transition,* except perhaps in the case of the Jewish Barmiztvah. We could say that the transition is **ritualized** through the various changes listed above. Many of these changes coincide with the transition to senior school where the roles and expectations are quite different from junior school. In some schools there are initiation rites that include bullying and degradation; there may also be an induction into the ethos and values of the new school: the colours, badges and mottoes. However, in many schools there is no symbolic rite of transition as uniforms are abolished and playing fields sold and schools close after the afternoon lessons. Some rituals are considered to be not politically correct, but they are not replaced by new ones. Some adolescents establish their own rituals of violence and the anti-hero, or drugs and substance abuse or food abuse and body disorders. Others drop out of school completely and find a subculture with its own rituals and rules and, where there are others like themselves – the peer group.

However it is done, the biggest transition for a child is that from parental dependency to peer group autonomy. As I have already mentioned, in a kibbutz the children are often at the centre and the adolescents at the margin, where they have relative freedom or freedom from relatives, to make decisions about their lives.

There are many dramas in this transitional time in relation to our emerging identity which can be tried and tested in the peer group. Indeed the influence of the peer group is so strong that parents are always cautioning against 'getting into bad company'. However, if adolescents can be helped to make this transition to a peer situation from a hierarchical one, they are well on their way to maturation. In adolescence, roles and images that manifested themselves in children's play are now tested in the gang in relation to the real world.

Although much of adolescence is one long drama, many young people eschew dramatic and artistic activities and look upon them as silly or weak or effeminate. The arts are considered a soft option and that's not for the lads. Luckily sport, for many, serves in the place of theatrical activity for both boys and girls. The school drama group seems to have many more girls in it than boys and one has to consider the threat inherent in it that makes young people feel so exposed. Adolescence itself is very exposing and many young people feel extremely vulnerable. Direct theatre activity for many is out of the question unless this process has already been central to them from earlier in their lives. Nevertheless, I have seen amazing work being done in drama by young people if the theme is important to them. I have seen adolescents tackle issues around drug, bullying and so on, as a piece of investigative drama. They have put tremendous energy into a documentary drama about a major theme that concerns them. But they have little time for imposed drama and theatre if it does not relate to their own lives and if they have not been involved before. It seems that for many young people we have to change the frame and enable them to dramatize events that hold meaning; events that can be made concrete through drama.

It is the same with rituals. Young people will invent rituals that have meaning for them rather than subscribe to rituals that seem outmoded and irrelevant. However, with music, sound and movement, with lights and costume, we are already in the performance world of young people. Time and resources must be made for them. We fortunately no longer live in a world, for the most part, where children and adolescents are made to do things without explanation or appreciation; now their own needs in terms of music and ritual can be addressed. It may not be our world or our music, but it is not meant to be so.

These are rites of separation from adults and it is important that difference is established even if initially it seems extreme. Maybe independence is only won by adolescents if they go right to the limits in total rebellion; then they can return with a new identity.

Obviously adults are necessary to facilitate the learning process, but so much of the learning can be done through drama and theatre. English literature, science, history and geography can all have an active ingredient whereby young people can investigate and dramatize. Many science museums and art galleries now have drama events for young people concerning inventions and technological developments. It is very encouraging that science brought alive through drama can have a long lasting effect on the learning process and difficult concepts can be understood through this interactive means, a true meeting of art and science which has so long been denied.

Drama can have an appropriate place both in the curriculum and in social development but it cannot be imposed. Where there is a strong drama tradition in a school and pupils attend the school because of this, then drama as an artistic medium can flourish as well.

Thus we can see that during this in between time of adolescence drama can be used to ritualize rebellion and contain change; that it can help to make sense or illuminate material both in curricula and culture; but perhaps most important it can facilitate and ritualize separation from parent and transition to peer. During this time the imagination is being severely tested in terms of our worlds and many young people play dramas continuously. Can you think of a better way to describe the search for identity? Self and reality are being constantly tested and roles are being experimented with. The paradox is, of course, that only through the capacity to separate completely can we tolerate closeness.

My definition of maturation is the capacity to distinguish every-day and dramatic reality and to be able to move in and out of each appropriately. Within this comprehension of two realities, maturity is also being able to tolerate closeness and difference as well as distance and similarity.

Perhaps this is what adolescence is all about and we need to allow young people to wander as well as return – to become 'hunter gatherers' and not just insist that they are 'settled cultivators'. Wandering is a necessary part of our development, and some of us wander for the whole of our lives. However, we live in a culture that expects us to 'settle down' in one place and have an address. Indeed to be 'of no fixed abode' is an indictment against our very personhood.

Exercises

The following questions may add to your own recollections of adolescent experience.

1. Can you recall celebrations for births, naming, coming of age, marriages and deaths? Were you a spectator or did you have a special role to play? Or to put it another way, did you have a peripheral or a central role in this special event? Please describe.

2. Describe any important bits of dreams and/or nightmares that you can recall at these stages. Were you playing a part in the dreams or were you the audience?

3. Write down times when you recall having imaginary conversations in your head or out loud. Did you answer yourself? Did you rehearse important events such as interviews in advance?

(If any memories start to flood back, just jot them down one at a time with key words.)

4. Describe your favourite daydream(s) and the role that you create for yourself in the daydream.

5. Are there important people in your life that perhaps are away from home or that have died, with whom you have had or are having private conversations?

(Some of the following questions you may like to enact or role-play with your co-dramatist, or perhaps use the appropriate voice and gesture.)

6. Do you enjoy telling stories about events that have happened in your present or past life? Do you just tell the facts or do you also use special voices, pauses for effect and dramatic punch lines?

7. Do you ever pretend to be someone else when you answer the telephone or when you open the door or make complaints?

8. Do you invent influential relatives or friends who will support you when in trouble? Do you ever create a family for yourself that is very different from the one you have?

You may like to look at your own notes and use a highlighter pen to mark any dramas where you have been **reality sorting**. Be aware of how your perceptions shift as you re-examine material that you held a particular view about. Keep remembering to put it all in context and not to hand-pick isolated incidents that perhaps maintain your theory.

CHAPTER FIVE

Drama, Ritualization and the Living of Life
'The need for knots'

In this chapter we shall look more objectively at the relationship between drama and adult life and thus the importance of dramatherapy if things get out of kilter. It is perhaps more difficult to look at life that is closer to ourselves in age and situation. Perhaps the recording of your own adult dramas can now be more fully processed and understood. Sometimes it takes a little longer. However, we shall need to consider some of the considerable prejudice that exists towards dramatic activity which is often based on misconceptions about what drama actually is. Many adults are unaware that they are engaging in dramatic activity for a large part of their daily life, and indeed have built on their own dramatic development to a greater or lesser extent. Some of the following statements have been made by adults about children and young people in relation to drama. I have chosen them deliberately to illustrate my theme of misconception

> Army Parent: 'My daughter doesn't need drama in order to understand what she is perfectly capable of understanding all ready.'

> Secondary School Head: 'Discipline is already a problem, give them drama and I shall have to call the police.'

> District Council Budget Meeting: 'Helping to fund a drama worker for the youth club would be just the beginning of non-essential demands on very scarce resources, and it would establish a precedent and open the floodgates.'

Rotarian Meeting: 'We are not being asked to give money for more children's scribbling and games are we?'

Hospital Manager: 'Of course it is important to provide activities for the patients but for the moment we can use our volunteers.'

Children's' Home Manager: 'Beryl, I don't want to stop you doing your...tambourine sessions with the children...but you must sort out your priorities.'

Funding For Inner City Projects: 'Don't mention drama in your application – call it something else.'

And I could go on! Adults in our society tend to look upon drama and playing as peripheral, childish activities that distract people from the really serious business of study, work and life itself. In many schools when exam revision starts, the drama classes are the first thing to be cancelled, yet in my view they should be increased to help deal with the stress that is engendered – perhaps for the staff, let alone the students. When people suggest that drama and theatre are not 'real' and therefore are unimportant, that is the very reason that they are important. Everyday life on its own is not enough, and it is only through the coexistence of dramatic reality that each of us can be truly a member of the human race and all that it entails.

Let us now look at adult dramatized and ritualized life and its relationship with the dramatized past. We will also consider the possibilities for change in people's lives through dramatherapy. Various themes have threaded through this book which illustrate how drama is central to the way in which we conduct our lives and how important it is for survival. Later we will consider them as core concepts in dramatherapy, here we will consider them in relation to the living of life in general.

Let us consider the contrast between a soap, that by its very design is closer to everyday life experience and indeed your own life (everyday reality); and a theatrical piece that is more distanced in structure, time and place, more remote from life, including your own (dramatic reality). I have found many people have an interesting contrast between the two forms. In the 'everyday drama', the less distanced form, people often have a close identification with a particular character or situation and have a strong emotional response to the various events that befell the character. For example, a scene and storyline concerning a woman being abandoned for another by the love of her life, brought recognition, tears and anger from people in similar situations:

> 'It was incredible – there was my life being played out before me – I felt just like that and there was nobody to be angry with...'

> 'I watch all the soaps because my life is in all of them – being fat, leaving home, falling out with the parents – you name it – I'm there!'

> 'I've stopped watching after they killed off my favourite character – I was devastated; how could they do that to me? It took me weeks to get over it. I sent flowers to the funeral.'

In soap drama, both on radio and television, audiences respond to the characters as real people – they write to them, give them advice, ring up about their health. They are not responding to the actors and actresses who play these characters but the characters themselves, and will call out the names of the characters if they happen to see them in the street. This does not usually happen in the theatre; an actor or actress is sent flowers or a card *for themselves rather than the character they are playing*. Thus cards are not sent to Ophelia or Hamlet or Katherine or Petruschio. In the soap the character and the performer, the story and everyday life are one and the same, there is no distancing. Of course it is a very powerful advertising message when our favourite characters endorse products in advertisements, sometimes even after they have died!

Thus you may find that there have been situations and relationships that remind you of your own life and perhaps you have had some strong feelings about them. You may have experienced similar feelings as the character or recognized your family or your boss. However has it changed anything? Has the fact that you have identified with the character changed your life? Has it empowered you to act in a new way? Do you look at your boss differently and try to communicate in a new way? Do you make allowances for your neighbour now because you realize she has problems herself?

The people I have talked with have said that in a way they find the soaps are very *reassuring* – here are people like ourselves who feel and think in the way we do. They speak on our behalf, and we can laugh and cry with them, but we do not feel different. I suggest that soaps are more about maintaining the *status quo* than about creating change. Furthermore, the ethical dilemmas and debates that take place in the episodes reflect society itself. We are taught what is right and wrong through the characters and even though there has been a welcome broadening of normative values regarding sex and gender, nevertheless, the moral code is one that we would all more or less adhere to.

The mechanisms of distancing not only involve the characters and contents that we see on the screen; they *are* also the actual location of the television and its small screen. The fact that we can switch on in our sitting rooms while doing other things such as eating, talking, revising, homework and so on, means that it has a closeness in its very situation that creates an intimacy. On the other hand in theatre you have to make a journey, sometimes for a long time, before you can even get to a theatre.

Unlike television, theatres are usually located some distance from where we live and for many people, not even in the same town. We can rarely just decide to go to the theatre; it has to be a planned event, tickets need to be booked and arrangements made to get home after a late night. Once we arrive there, it always takes time to get inside; do we leave our coats, order a drink for the interval, buy a programme? Do we like our seat? How much do we know about the play? All these issues before a play has even started. Similarly, when we leave the theatre, it always takes time; we can never leave in a hurry so we make a slow transition into the outside world.

Different theatre practitioners have suggested that various things happen to us in a theatre – is it to make us think or is it to make us feel? Is it to take us out of ourselves or is it to take us into ourselves? Is it to clarify or confuse? Does it endorse or challenge? I suspect that all these things are probably happening to us at one time or another while a play is unfolding in front of us. However, without question there are various mechanisms that actually contribute to the distancing, such as the elements of time, place, character and scene. Even when playwrights and directors attempt 'naturalistic theatre' or 'realism', or the performance is a promenade one where the audience moves about or sits in the round, or when there are attempts to re-create an actual life event, we are still entering an 'as if' situation. We have to put on one side the logical, rational left hemisphere of our brains and enter into a fictive situation in a spirit of believing what we see; we know it is not 'real' and we know it is performers creating on our behalf and inviting us to witness. If we are engaged with the piece then we are transported out of our everyday selves into the dramatic reality of the theatre; and we stay within this reality more or less until the end. We may surface if there is an interval, we are jolted if there are serious mistakes, such as performers forgetting their lines or scenery falling over, but at the end of the piece we start to come back to ourselves as we applaud the performers who are now out of character.

As we walk away from a theatre we may feel a range of feelings and think a range of thoughts. If it is a familiar play such as one of Shakespeare's, we may want to ponder a new interpretation; we may hear a phrase we have never heard before; we realize that a relationship we saw from one perspective can also be seen from the opposite.

Shakespeare was a jobbing actor who wrote for the stage and it is in performance that we make our discoveries. The scenes and stories are not of our everyday lives and the characters are not those of our street – and never were. The language is very different and has always been so, BUT the plays still find a resonance with us in quite different ways. The dilemmas and relationships that are enacted before us are symbolic of all the relationships that we have ever encountered, and the issues being debated are the issues that have always preoccupied people over history. The stories involve all classes of people and all themes of love, hate, jealousy, family feuds and corruption of the state; dream life and war life; ancient myth and poetic fable. Furthermore, the language of these plays is the language of metaphor and image and symbol and it is this language that enters our own consciousness and makes an impact on our thought systems. Dominant symbols in any culture are those symbols with multiple meanings and associations that are central to rituals and rites; they impact upon us in ways that we cannot usually articulate. These symbolic and metaphoric statements together with the lighting and sound and design and music and movement all alert the senses and thought processes in ways that are not possible in the world and language of the everyday. It affects us differently and enables us to experience something in the reality of the theatre. Paradoxically, the distancing mechanisms serve to bring us closer to ourselves.

The world of the theatre is the microcosm of the world itself, and through this small world of the theatre, we ourselves become connected to the world itself. A cosmological experience in the true sense of the word.

In my discussions with people concerning this book they have talked about theatre prompting them to think in new ways and that it has brought about change in their lives, not in a reactive way but in a way that has enabled them to give thought and balance to various issues that need considering. The context of the theatre has allowed them to put their life into context and as one person said to me, 'I have found my life on the map at last – it is very worrying when you don't see yourself there'.

Theatre is about great stories that we may encounter in new and different ways or stories that we are hearing for the first time. Some theatre we may feel quite disconnected from and other we may feel does not transport us anywhere. Nevertheless we never leave a theatre in a neutral frame of mind, there is always something that has made an impact. I concentrate on Shakespeare because my own belief is that it is through his plays that the most obvious processes of change to which I am referring can be experienced. But the same processes are felt through the ancient plays of Greece and playwrights throughout the ages – Molière, Ibsen, Chekhov, Lorca, Pirandello, Pinter, Churchill, to name but a few. Rather than debate individual playwrights, I want to comment on types of live theatre. Does a performance of *The Mousetrap* 'work' in the same way as one of the classics? *The Mousetrap* is rather like a soap or police TV drama which creates a realistic story, and although it is to some extent distanced simply because it is in the theatre, its language and characterization are nevertheless very near to our own experience. We are entertained, we experience suspense, we may identify with a character or event, but does it bring about change?

Television soaps and some theatre forms impact on us in quite different ways, and in some ways complement each other. The soaps reassure us, reinforce where we are at, whereas the theatre can challenge us and often provoke us to reconsider something.

You may completely disagree, but examine these statements in the light of your own life events and tease out your opinion of your relationship to television and theatre and your life. If you have a drama partner you may also disagree with each other, and this will also assist you in forming your own ideas and clarifying what you think. My role is that of a provocateur!

The ritualization of life events is another means of creating dramatic form and structure which is closely linked to theatre but is also distinguishable from it. There is not a society which does not ritualize certain events concerning change, belief and celebration. When we ritualize an event, we are making a symbolic statement in a dramatic form that has a common language which is understood by the participants. We may analyze a ritual into its various component parts and discuss layers of meaning that may not necessarily be available to the participants; in other words they have not stood outside it and considered it as separate from their own experience of the ritual.

Rituals are shared events that are usually enacted by a specific group of people who are connected through belief to others who witness the ritual.

This contrasts with theatre where the witnessing group or audience is far more random, and where the content may provoke change rather than make a symbolic statement. Rituals are also about transitions from one social state to another so they guide us through changes in a very specific way. Rituals of birth and death, coming of age and so on, enable us to let go of our current role and status and be affirmed in the new role and status. For example, when we participate in a marriage celebration, as guests we witness the letting go of the single status of the couple and their transition into a shared status with its accompanying rights and obligations. Whether it is a religious ritual or a civil one, there are legal and contractual agreements that are publicly stated. Special costumes are worn by the central characters as well as the audience, and there is a ritual form to the event which includes music and readings, often from ancient texts. There is the ritualized giving of gifts for the shared home and the renaming of both the couple and their close relatives. There is special food that is eaten and also sent to those people unable to attend in person. The ritual does not end with either the ceremony or the party but continues into the first months of joint life, often accompanied by practical jokes, bawdy comments and a rearrangement of life in relation to working, socializing, considerations of children and so on. We may feel that a particular wedding is very theatrical in its presentation and indeed it may well have many theatrical elements, but the central characters are enacting this piece which, although symbolic in form, has legal implications and certain expectations of outcome.

Have there been occasions where you attended a ritual even though the underlying religion or belief was not one to which you could adhere? Did it still have an impact on you, and was the event significant for you in relation to the people playing the central characters? If you were a central character, how did you make the decisions concerning the particular ritual form that you chose?

Throughout this book so far, I have emphasized the importance of certain forms of live theatre that are important for change and development in us as human beings, and have indicated that this can be applied when needed as a therapeutic intervention. I also said in earlier chapters that there are other dramatic forms such as film and television that can serve a similar purpose, albeit in varying ways. However, it is the underlying dramatic processes that we have experienced in our lives that form the bedrock on which these experiences are built. The most important of these are the growth of the dramatic imagination and the maturation into understanding the everyday and dramatic realities. This enables us to develop empathy and conscience and to have a mechanism through which we can process our life events. This process I have referred to as the re-working of experience. We have talked about how we need to tell stories and events especially if they have had a profound effect on us. We take on the various characters and voices and re-tell the story in many different ways. In recording your own history and telling it to someone else, you will have 're-worked' some of it. You will have told the tale as you remember, not just as a story but in an enacted form. There will be different characters and dramatic pauses and some instances of dramatic effect. Re-working events to others enables us to make sense of them and to see them from different points of view; indeed in the telling we will use different emphases depending on our audience. Sometimes we can be stuck at an event that creates a one-dimensional view of our experience. Generally speaking I do not find that the literal re-working of a past event is particularly helpful; like the soap it can be reassuring but often just maintains the *status quo*. It takes a bigger step of using theatre or dramatherapy to have sufficient distance and metaphor to enable it to be experienced in a different way.

Dramatic re-working of experience is something we all do in our lives as we tell tales that have recently happened to us. If a re-working has not taken place at the time, being stuck can create distortion and misperception.

A more distanced form of theatre, constructed in the present, is usually more truthful in helping to resolve such situations and it will also provide choices of outcome.

Although we are adept at re-working our own lives in various ways, when we rework other people's lives it is called gossip! I am a great believer in gossip within its rightful context. It is a source of information and enables information to be passed on; it allows us to have fantasies about people unknown to us and partake in their dramas, and it is also a powerful restraint on behaviour. There are many things we do not do 'because people will talk'; therefore gossip can be seen to regulate what we do. However, when gossip becomes malicious, salacious or invented, it becomes what I've called mischief drama. A picture of a friend of mine appeared in a newspaper with someone else's body attached to her head, which completely distorted what was being said about her. A picture of me appeared on the front of the *Evening Standard* which had been taken at a dramatherapy workshop for doctors working in fertility clinics where we used fertility symbols, including an enormous wooden snake. The picture showed only me and the snake and was used to illustrate a controversial statement that had been made by another person with a similar name. Again the statement was completely distorted, exaggerated by a picture taken out of its context. This, I suggest, is 'mischief drama' and does not enhance or educate or regulate but ultimately detracts and damages.

Not only can malicious gossip damage, drama itself can be used in ways that are unhelpful to the participants and at times are harmful. I remember at the college where I taught dramatherapy there used to be a slogan that art therapy might be messy but dramatherapy was downright dangerous! Drama can be misused as a technique in the theatre as well as in education and in therapy. Once someone is engaged in the drama process it is very easy to implant ideas, create auto-suggestion, manipulate memories and re-create a personality. This is why it is essential that people are properly trained in the use of drama methods and that they also examine their own motives for using drama. It is unacceptable to want to assert power over other people by making them very vulnerable through the drama.

As I wrote earlier, I have been aware of the fierce debate concerning suppressed memory. There is currently much debate about multiple-selves versus false memory syndrome, and I am concerned about the misuse of role-playing to 'discover' so called buried selves. Some therapists use regressive techniques to 'uncover' hidden experiences that are suggested to be impeding growth. However, we all know how easy it is to create a fictional past for ourselves. We know through our own dramatized history that we have given ourselves identities and actions that perhaps were exaggerated or even fictive. That is all part of our imagination. If we are unhappy we can cheer ourselves up by creating a character for ourselves and allow that character to have adventures. But to focus on the idea that there are traumatic abusive events in our past that have not been addressed, and to dramatize them out of the context of our lives as a whole is, I think, a most dangerous way of approaching therapy. This is not to suggest that all such buried memories are fictive.

Nonetheless, in my approach to therapy, I think that it is far more important to deal with the health of now and to find ways of working in the two realities. How otherwise do we guard against the dramatic imagination reconstructing a past event instead of our everyday memory? At what level do we 'know' that something happened to us or not? Sometimes in psychotherapy we tell the therapist things that we think they want to know when they assume that there is a major event in our past that has made us neurotic in the present. But how does anyone know? What, beyond therapeutic speculation, proves that a past trauma that has been repressed is affecting us now? Because of our very talent in re-creating fictions for ourselves, I would suggest that to concentrate on discovering the reality of the past, over and above our conscious memory and actual documentation, is not very constructive. I think it more helpful to work in the dramatic reality in the here and now, and to create scenes with themes and metaphors that seem to relate to our life story within the bigger story of myths and plays. This approach does not ignore a person's troubled past but helps them find a means of exploring it through distancing and the dramatic imagination. My life now needs to be in the context of my life as a whole, together with the lives of those people that have been around me in the past present and future.

So far in this chapter I have discussed dramatic distancing and the two realities and the way in which they affect our dramatic relationship with the world. We have also looked at how certain life events are ritualized within a belief system and our part in those rituals, and we have contrasted ritual with theatre. I reiterated the importance of the development of the dramatic imagination and how it helps the re-working of life experience in dramatic form. I suggested that gossip is when we rework the lives of others. However, I also cautioned against the misuse of role playing to uncover a hypothesized or imagined past under the guise that it was a real event. I now want to move onto the part of this book that is perhaps the most difficult for me to write; this is the whole question of drama and the development of conscience – in other words a moral code.

Once we start to experience as a child the ability to be 'other' (and as we saw this starts with our being able to talk to the toy and then role-reverse with it), we are able to go beyond self and the needs of the self. We experience the beginnings of conscience which means that we begin to understand some form of moral code; that is, we start to know the difference between 'good and bad' or 'right and wrong'. It may be considered very old fashioned to use this type of language and even to consider the notion of a moral code. However, I maintain that everything we do is underpinned by a belief system or ethical principles. Usually these have evolved collectively and not individually, because they have been found to work, in other words they make it possible for the individuals in a society to lead their lives reasonably effectively. Just because some systems of belief or ideology have been abused and certain groups of people have suffered oppression, is not to say that an ethical code does not work. I do not believe that we are helped by the view that as long as it feels right for me then it must be all right. Sometimes therapy is described as 'sorting out myself', and I have talked earlier about how, in individual therapy, a person can be 'sorted out' at the expense of others, and often to their detriment. Again and again, I come back to this view that individuals exist in relation to others, and that any impact on one will have an impact on the others. At the very least, the 'confessional' took into account the context and the code, which are not usually present in psychotherapy.

Perhaps I am actually challenging the notion that any regard for another can or indeed should be unconditional. Any view of this world and the people in it has my own conditions and limitations. These I hope are tempered by my capacity to empathize, which may ameliorate how I feel, but does not therefore make it unconditional.

Too often I hear statements such as the following:

'It doesn't feel right for me to do this'

'The word "should" oppresses me'

'No one can make me do anything'

I was criticized for grouping a course reading-list under the following headings: essential texts, recommended texts and general reading. I was asked to regroup them under: indicative reading, support reading. I compromised and used the headings: core texts and further reading. I was told that to say that a text was essential was too prescriptive and could be experienced as oppressive. The difficulty with trying to create a neutral language is that we end up saying nothing at all.

There are, however, other ways in which we become members of a social group and adhere to the norms and values necessary for that group to function. When I conducted fieldwork in Malaysia I was struck how the ethnic group with whom I carried out my research appeared to have a reasonably balanced view of the relationship between the individual and the group. They would say to me that you cannot impose your will on another, that people do what they want, that this person can choose what he or she wants to do, that parents cannot make their children do something. In the next sentence they would give me their moral code of behaviour, to which it was important to adhere; that to be a good member of the group you should behave in certain ways and not in others; that you must know the old ways because that tells you what to do. They seemed to prescribe an individual freedom and a group responsibility at one and the same time. Parents are very indulgent to their children and do not use physical chastisement to enforce rules and regulations. The agents of punishment are thunder and tiger, and children have a fear response to both these larger-than-life agents from the world of nature. The natural world spirits from the souls of plants that are kindly and are bringers of health and healing are, by contrast, small and shy compared with the size and loud noise of tiger and thunder. These shy spirits also act as role models for people in terms of how human beings should behave; in other words, they should not draw attention to themselves, especially when they are in the forest or river, or when they are newly returned to their villages.

By contrast, loud and noisy behaviour is allowed in their trance dramas, which are enacted regularly both for health as well as for healing. There is loud music and singing and people stagger about in trance, often collapsing and even falling through the floor. Although these dramas are in contrast to their more sedate everyday behaviour, nevertheless the noise and flailing of limbs is still expressed within certain limits; even loss of control is structured. The value system supports the practicalities of living in a subsistence forest environment where the development of the senses in terms of survival is essential. If your hearing and sight are not acute then you will neither find enough food to eat nor will you be aware of potential dangers to your person. However their role models are not only in the spirit world; parents and other adults present models of appropriate behaviour rather than 'do as I say not as I do'. Children do not see adults hit each other or shout insults or abuse; anger is quiet and restrained rather than demonstrated in an obvious way. The physical hurt or killing of others is anathema and even the slaughter of certain animals for food has to be undertaken away from human habitation and is surrounded by ritualized food preparation rules, and is only allowed to be eaten by certain classifications of people. By the time that animal meat is brought into the village, it has undergone a transformation so that it does not look like the animal anymore.

I am not suggesting that this way of dealing with child rearing and a moral code is appropriate for our culture or that we should impose this way of life on ourselves. This system has evolved appropriate to the people concerned over many centuries. I describe it to show that there are other ways to consider an ethical system, and ones in which there are strong ideas of how people behave towards others. Furthermore, this particular society continuously create and dramatize their life events and start this process at a very young age. Children as young as two years old are already taking on adult roles not only in family scenes but also in the trance drama scenes that they witness. People describe the contents and dramatic forms of their dreams, many of which are thought to have predictive validity in terms of searching for food or discovering a new cure or learning a new dance. The dreams that people talked about were dreams of use to others. Maybe they had others that they did not choose to divulge!

Many moral systems are oppressive and are imposed from without and, furthermore, may not be questioned. Rote learning of creeds and codes often indoctrinate without any true understanding, and explanations are frowned upon. However, it was the early churches that encouraged role-playing and dramas as part of learning about religion, and indeed the very first play in our culture was four lines long, and was part of the Easter Mass. Some of the travelling monks that took cures to the highways and byways used drama and storytelling to encourage people to take their medicine. There is a medieval text of cures that is called 'Theatricum Sanitum' and of course we still refer to an operating theatre.

Figure 5.1 The Odysseus workshop in Israel: The Hydra

Figure 5.2 The Odysseus workshop in Denmark: The Hydra

Figure 5.3 The Odysseus workshop in Denmark: The Cyclops

We need to look at the actual process whereby we can acquire a moral sense, i.e. through the act of drama. We can then see that it is learned through playing and the capacity to be other than ourselves. We learn about the outcome of our actions on others and because we are beginning to discover empathy, we are able to know that we can hurt someone, and also how that hurt feels. We have discovered it for ourselves rather than just being told what to do. We have developed the capacity not just to be ourselves but to be otherselves and therefore to be able to go beyond ourselves. Surely this is how we are able to acquire the experience and perception to be able to do more than just survive in the world.

Figure 5.4 The Odysseus workshop in Denmark. Odysseus, tied to the mast, sets off – the integration of embodiment, projection and role.

Figure 5.5 The Odysseus workshop in Denmark. The Syrens' temptation.

The dramatic imagination and the ensuing testing and trying out of roles and scenarios needs to be constantly developed throughout our lives, not just when we play as small children. This process leads into cultural forms of ritual and art, including music, dance and visual art, but in particular theatre art. Theatre art can in fact incorporate all art forms in a performative event so that it synthesizes the verbal and non-verbal as well as being able to resonate at multiple levels.

If we have not had extensive dramatic experience as children it does not mean that we shall always be at a disadvantage. You will see from the questionnaires at the end of the book that in fact there are many things we can do to balance our everyday and our dramatic experience. There will be many ways that I have not mentioned that are satisfying to you and I know that when you and your Ariadne discuss it jointly, you will act as a trigger for each other.

The more we can do drama the more we will be able to do. It is not a question of staying within the dramatic reality more and more because 'that way madness lies'. The more opportunities that we give ourselves to practise being 'other' by entering roles and scenes, rather than just imagining it, the more we will expand in relation to ourselves and others.

It is through this ever expanding sense of self and other within a creative frame of dramatic expression that we perhaps can find some type of fulfilment – even a challenging one – in an albeit imperfect world.

Exercises

Take a sheet of paper and write a summary of your own drama experience **as if you are someone else observing yourself**. You could be a parent or a teacher or a 'significant other person'; or just the notion of someone other than yourself. You are writing about yourself in the third person. You are in fact role reversing with an other which, as we shall see, is the primary act of drama that is talked about in ensuing chapters.

> *When you have done this, read it to your co-dramatist, or role-play this other person, saying the things you have written. I am sure you will find more things to write down in your history once you have done this exercise. You may then create a role chart concerning the significant people in your past life who were for and against, you and drama and theatre.*

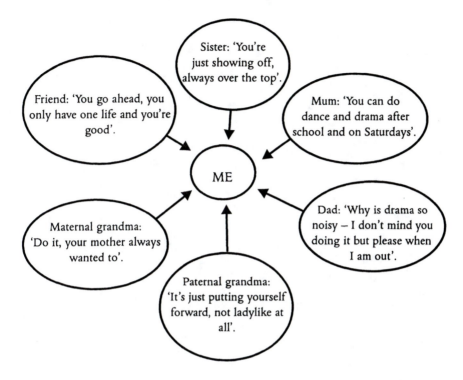

Figure 5.6 Role chart 3

Use a new page and place yourself in the centre and group these other people around you. This role chart is purely to look at other people's attitudes towards you participating in drama and theatre (there are many different rolecharts we can create about our lives).

Having created this chart, repeat the different phrases in the voices of the people who said them. How many voices can you actually own as being yours rather then other people's? Go back and re-read the summary your wrote about your life. Whoever you thought was writing it, it actually is your self creating this summary. Allow yourself to acknowledge the fact.

CHAPTER SIX

Dramatherapy Core Concepts
'The thread has led us through the maze'

In the previous chapters we have found that through our own experience and by looking at observable phenomena in the human world, a plethora of scenes stand out that, within my definition, we can call dramatic. To put it another way, we have both done and seen actions and interactions that are in a theatrical structure in the reality of the dramatic imagination; that is, that do not belong to everyday factual experience. Let us look more objectively now at the thread which has led us through the dramatherapy maze and consider the core concepts of dramatherapy.

1. Theatrical distance

When we witness a piece of theatre, or participate in a theatrical experience, it is distanced from our everyday life. As audience we metaphorically sit back from an artistic exposition that is being enacted or re-enacted in front of us. Landscapes and scenes are presented to us, the willing spectators, as stories unfold. If we participate in the enactment, we step into the reality of the drama as a character within a narrative that is not our own character or narrative. There may be connections, direct and indirect, but the whole experience is distanced from our own experience because of the very devices that make it theatre.

We physically enter a building or space that is set apart for theatre and there are designated places for us to sit or stand. There are conventions about this space which vary between cultures but which usually govern the way we dress, whether we can eat food, make a noise, respond to the piece and so on. In most western theatres the audience sits in semi-darkness while the acting space is illuminated. We may have programmes which describe the piece, and the actors and others who are involved in the performance. There may be an interval when the consumption of drinks and snacks is allowed and people can walk around. It is now a thing of the past when you would order your tray of tea for the interval of a matinee and the programme sellers would bring your tray to where you were sitting. In most plays we can see the shape of the theatrical structure where an interval is at a point of tension in the play, which is then usually resolved in the second half. Spotlights and lamps illuminate and fade, curtains open and close, the safety curtain is visible at least once during the evening, and the changes of costume and special effects are some of the means through which the experience is distanced from us. As an actor we inhabit these different characters, wearing costumes, make-up, and masks which distance the experience both for ourselves and the audience. We are aware of the artifice of the props and scenery, the contrived 'business' and magical tricks that are all part of the experience; and we know that at most only ninety per cent of us can be involved, because our other consciousness has to be alert to the structure of the play, the other characters and the furniture on the set. Actor and audience enter an alliance of distance through which a story can be told.

The paradox of this distance is that both actor and audience come closer not just to each other but to the themes and characters of the plot and subplots. Images, metaphors and subtexts resonate for us as we are guided through this theatrical journey being communicated within the dramatic reality.

As individuals as well as a collective audience we enter this dramatic reality and are by turns scared, angry, touched as the piece moves us. As the actors meet the audience they too experience not only the nuances of the character, but the way it is shaped by this audience; performers and audience feed off each other in this joint enterprise. At the end there are again conventions through which we separate from the theatrical involvement; the curtain call brings us back from the piece as we applaud the actors who are still in their costumes but stand there as themselves. We are applauding them and not their characters, and then the lights come up and we have to wait patiently to get out of the theatre.

Although there are variations on this, such as the way we respond to a play we do not like, or the convention that baddie pantomime characters are booed at the curtain call, the above is more or less a description of a theatre performance within the western convention. We walk away from the theatre with 'special moments' resonating for us, and these will often continue to resonate for days and weeks to come.

The paradox of theatrical distancing is that we can come closer to issues that concern us and our lives, both as individuals as well as the world as a whole.

2. The two realities

In the perception of our everyday concrete world, forays into our imagination are often called fantasy. Psychotherapists in particular see any speculation about life and living as fantasy; I remember at a conference when a colleague said to me, 'What is your fantasy about dinner tonight?'

I think it is both more accurate and less confusing if we consider the fact that there are at least two realities: the reality of our day-to-day experience and the reality of our dramatic imagination. There are no doubt that other realities or truths exist, such as poetic truth, for example; but the two realities that concern us here are everyday reality and dramatic (or theatrical) reality. We enter the dramatic reality when we say 'let's pretend we are monsters' or 'I am reacting as if I have just heard bad news' or 'imagine you are on a beach in Greece'.

When we explored our own dramatic development and observed how infants and children play we saw the emergence of dramatic reality; and how young children often confuse the 'actual' with the 'let's pretend'. As children grow up they are able to distinguish these two realities more and more accurately, and sadly much of our education system is about encouraging factual assimilation and discouraging the creative imagination.

My definition of maturation is the capacity to distinguish every-day and dramatic reality and to be able to move in and out of each appropriately.

The polarization between 'the arts' and 'the sciences' is an artificial one since both types of thinking are important, and are not necessarily separate. If we could not take a dramatic leap of the imagination into the unknown, then we could never form a hypothesis. I would suggest that great scientists must have an overdeveloped dramatic imagination in order to speculate about how something might be before returning to their laboratories to see if it is possible.

Psychologists refer to the brain as having two major hemispheres: the left hemisphere is for numeracy, logic, facts; the right is for creativity, symbols, metaphors and the imagination. To function as fully as possible we need to be able to move across these hemispheres and allow one to stimulate the other. This is why our education throughout life needs to be in both these hemispheres rather than the emphasis on one at the expense of the other. Science and technology are given priority in our education system, and the arts and creativity are not supported by staffing or funding. Yet we find that far more young people try to enter artistic courses after they leave school than technological ones. I suggest that applied theatre can assist in learning all subjects including the sciences and creative thinking is essential for all tasks. My own theatre work which explores women in medicine and science has been performed for pupils as young as eight years old, and they concentrated and were absorbed, much to the amazement of their teachers.

Let us look at the theoretical implications of these two realities in relation to applied dramatherapy, particularly in a clinical setting and illustrate it with examples. First I want to look at our understanding of pathology itself in relation to dramatherapy concepts, especially my notion of everyday reality and dramatic reality.

Traditional clinicians would suggest that creative activities and especially drama were unsuitable for people suffering from certain mental health problems. In particular it was suggested that people diagnosed as psychotic or borderline would become worse if they did drama:

> 'what they need is a good dose of reality' as one psychiatrist said to me, 'all this fantasy business could be very dangerous and even push them over the edge'.

Clinicians often think that the main task of mental health treatments is to make people 'functional' in order to survive in the everyday world. In earlier chapters, we discovered that dramatic reality is also important in relation to survival, and there were times in our own lives when an imaginary friend or an active day dream enabled us to tolerate difficulties in the everyday world. However it is important, especially for vulnerable people, that these two realities are maintained as separate worlds albeit worlds that inter-connect. It can be unhelpful when the borders around these realities become blurred.

Despite early clinical scepticism, dramatherapy has been found to be a very effective means of working with people with severe mental health issues. There are clinicians who specialize in working with short-term dramatherapy with severely unwell people and have been surprised at the changes.

Let us look here at the possibility of the two realities themselves being used as diagnostic tools. A person who is borderline or diagnosed as psychotic is often described as being out of touch with reality, of being cut off from their own experience, of losing their own identity. He or she may hear voices or assume another identity or carry out movements or make sounds that appear inappropriate to the context in which they are placed. If this all took place within the context of a dramatic scene we would not take issue with it. The person experiences these phenomena **as if** it is their everyday reality; the borders between the everyday and the dramatic have dissolved, as indeed can happen with actors who are over-immersed in their characters.

People who are described as being borderline or psychotic could be described as people who are trapped in dramatic reality.

For whatever reason, they are unable to move in and out of the two realities as described above. They seem out of touch with their everyday experience and an identity, and function in an assumed role and setting.

The careful application of dramatherapy is a most appropriate means of re-establishing borders round the dramatized experience that has become uncontained and dysfunctional. It is possible to work with all modes of dramatherapy described in this book in order to separate out and make transitions between the two realities. The Odyssey project that I mentioned earlier is an apt example. In this psychiatric hospital there were fears by staff that their patients would become more unwell as a result of the dramatherapy, especially when they knew that the story contained a scene of Odysseus's journey to the underworld to talk to his mother. I was asked to cut that scene. The interesting point was that all the patients wanted to re-enact that scene after they had seen the dramatized story. I set very clear borders that it was **Odysseus going to talk to his mother** and there was careful de-roling afterwards with discussion and the transition from dramatic reality to everyday reality. Clinical opinion was that this patient group had never been so lucid.

If I am confused in my thinking and orientation in role and reality, dramatherapy through playing 'the other' can help me reach some order in my experience.

Let us now consider another diagnostic category, the person who has a personality disorder. Most commonly within this frame is the person who has a psychopathic personality or who is a psychopath. The former could be the simple con-person who knocks on your door and tricks you into parting with money or possessions for an enterprise that does not exist. You might think that they are extremely good actors, which is true. However there is a big but: their 'acting' does not take place in dramatic reality but in everyday reality. Moment to moment is a continuous drama with assumed identities, voices, stories and so on.

At the other extreme, the psychopath, for example the serial killer, lives out a high drama as his or her everyday life. If the actions were part of a Greek Tragedy, we should not take issue with them, but they are being perpetrated in everyday life: the killings are done for real and not symbolically. There is no 'as if' in these actions.

People who are described as psychopaths or has having a psychopathic personality, could be described as being trapped in everyday reality.

They are unable to move in and out of dramatic reality, and turn their everyday life into a permanent drama. It is usually said that such people do not have a developed conscience, which is another way of saying that they are unable to understand the implications of the outcome of their actions. I shall consider in more detail the development of conscience and the important part that drama has in this, later in this chapter.

I am not suggesting that dramatherapy can 'cure' someone who is labelled a psychopath but I know, at the very least, that it came make them more aware of the outcome of what they have done. In my work with offender patients, the enactment of a story through text seems to heighten the participant's awareness of outcome. For example in an Odyssey project with this patient group there were two scenes which seemed to resonate more that the others. The first was the scene with the Syrens when each patient made a Syren mask and talked through the mask of what tempted Odysseus away from his journey. One patient wore the mask and said, 'when you see me from a distance, I am all spring and summer, but when you come near me I am autumn and winter and icy cold'.

The other scene was the return to Ithaca, to Odysseus' homeland. Where was home? Was it within the hospital or our former home or was it in our heads? 'A land too stony for horses' had a personal and symbolic meaning for all the patient group and they linked it to the exploration they had done of 'special trees' (the rooted image) in an earlier dramatherapy group. There was a most moving moment in the story when Odysseus returned home and the question was, would he be recognized and initially he wasn't. It was his old nurse that recognized his scar who was the first person to know him.

Let us now move on to the third major concept in dramatherapy.

3. Embodiment–Projection–Role: the drama developmental paradigm

In earlier chapters we saw how the EPR development in human beings is embedded virtually from conception onwards and how these three stages are established by about the age of seven years. We also saw how the stages continue to be re-visited throughout our lives with eventual preference for one mode or another. For example the professional dancer eventually focuses on embodiment as his or her main mode of being whereas the aerobics teacher, although strongly in embodiment, in fact is more focused in projection, since teaching of all kinds is largely a projective activity. No-one is solely in a single mode but has a predominance in their work and leisure; in fact for many people, leisure can balance out the focus of the work life. Although this book is mainly about artistry and artistic activity, and drama and theatre in particular, we can find EPR patterning and its various combinations in all activities to a greater or lesser extent. Indeed an analysis of a person's EPR preferences could assist in career choices and life changes. Here though we are specifically concerned with the drama developmental mode being applied as a structure for dramatherapy.

Since EPR is an observed and accurate developmental progress in life itself, we can take it as a structure for applied dramatherapy. It is a structure that is easily learnt by facilitators and facilitates themselves There are many people in treatment settings who have not progressed through these stages in their younger life or have become stuck through shock or trauma in a single stage. In particular many people seem to have missed out on the embodiment, the E stage. The answer is not to start immediately with lots of energetic E or your client group will head for the door. It may mean that you start with something far less direct such as projection, the P or that some E is designed that is not scary.

For example, some groups of people are very anxious about moving round the room and find security in sitting in chairs; yet many of them join in an evening of social dancing, enjoy dressing up for the event and have no difficulties dealing with the physical contact that is the convention in such dance. Therefore we have to consider that it is the unfamiliarity that causes the anxiety in the dramatherapy. It is important to start with familiar EPR elements before moving into the unfamiliar experiences. **Any dramatherapy content is a mixture of the known and the unknown, or the ritual and the risk, or the home base and the adventure.**

It may be that any movement causes anxiety for people so consider starting with projection; P. Working with creativity outside the self, *away* from ourselves, rather than *with* ourselves is less intimidating for many people and may enable them to feel more in control. A games of consequences is a projective game and familiar to most people. It is also intrinsically dramatic as it is about creating imaginary and fantastic characters who do things and could simple lead into physical expression or role work. Dramatherapy does not have to be complicated.

> **People will respond to situations and ideas that are familiar, and that have delighted them in the past. They will approach with awe events that are 'beyond' them, or with consternation activities that might make them feel stupid.**

However, whatever the anxiety or ability levels in your groups, they will be greatly enhanced if you and your group can sit down and plan the dramatherapy. As I said earlier, the more you can preserve some autonomy, the healthier your clients will become. You can build and enhance and develop on whatever your clients suggest so that they feel within the frame too.

> **Dramatherapy should not be a mystery and people should not be asked to enter into an experience that they do not fully understand. They should have opportunities to both question and discuss.**

> **People readily grasp dramatic principles when they are given examples, and especially when they have the opportunity to record their own dramatized history.**

4. Dramatic re-working of experience

We have seen how we are constantly dramatizing experiences that we need to deal with. Something happens to us and we re-tell it in dramatic form, taking on postures and gestures, changing our voice and playing out roles. We usually do this to an audience and will vary our act as our audience varies. Sometimes we will do it for an imaginary audience and enact the scene in our heads or out loud in privacy. Re-working seems to be an important activity which enables us to move on in our lives. When people come for therapy, we may find that they have become stuck at a particular event that they were unable to re-work. Instead of moving on, they keep repeating the event in many variations, or repeat their coping mechanisms for dealing with the event. We could consider all forms of addiction in this way as people struggle to control their destiny however destructive it may seem to the concerned observer.

Food, alcohol, drugs, mutilation, sex, all have addictive forms where they are decontextualized and where new rituals are created around the addiction. All are concerned with the physical body and all have socially acceptable variations.

In my experience, if re-working has not taken place in the aftermath of the event itself, acting out the event does not necessarily assist the process. However, if the event is part of a distanced drama and theatre piece, it seems that this enables the re-working to take place in a different form.

For example, with a group of people with severe mental health problems, we were working on the story of Jacob's Ladder from the Old Testament. First we told the story and then created scenes which included the journey through the desert, the vision of the ladder and angels, and the creation of Jacob's house. Everyone could choose their roles and people were stones in the desert, angels, parts of the ladder, and parts of the house, as well as Jacob himself. Several people were very 'stuck' and although involved in various long term therapies seemed to have some difficulties in 'moving on'. Part of the de-roling from the dramatherapy is to give feedback as the character before ones gives feedback as oneself and the following statements are examples of the depth of people's experience.

'as the stone, I realised I had been stuck for many years'

'as the ladder I felt very strong which was a new feeling'

'as part of the House of Jacob I felt connected to everyone in the group'.

It was the staff that found this piece of dramatherapy work more difficult than the patients, and seemed to find difficulty in allowing people to make their own responses. Two members of staff hid under blankets and said they were role-modelling for the patients. Now there is a paradox!

5. Dramatic structure of the mind

Since we have considered the many forms that our dramas may take and the very early start of their development, let us now consider the possibility of a dramatic structure of the mind. This perhaps feels an enormous leap, and it could be that the various internal states that I am about to describe are called by different terminology in other disciplines. However, perceiving these states as dramatic not only helps us understand our own dramatic processes but has also proved useful as a diagnostic tool when designing appropriate programmes of dramatherapy.

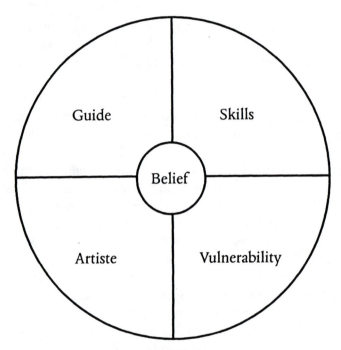

Figure 6.1 Dramatic Structure of the Mind

The above rather simplistic divisions nevertheless give us four major areas of personhood for want of a better word: everybody has their internal skills, their internal guide, their internal artiste and their internal vulnerability, and a state of being in the world comes about from an interplay between these states. Mediated through our belief system, these states make up a totality of being a person and they feed and stimulate each other. To have internal skills is not just that we have skills in certain areas but to know and experience that we are skilled, even if we are not practising such skills. Our internal guide is that part of ourselves that can stand outside and monitor what we are doing in a benign way. Our internal artiste is our creative and artistic self that can create in its own right but also stimulates other areas. Our vulnerability is always there and needs support from the other states, and it is important that we know we are vulnerable, even if we choose not to show it. These four states develop through our dramatic growth, together with our emergent belief system, which may be a formal religion or philosophy or set of values concerning what we hold to be right and wrong. Remember how I described in the Introduction when Jiminy Cricket says, 'What does an actor need with a conscience?' Indeed this echoes some very deep misgivings about the nature of drama and it was Plato who felt that a good actor should be driven out of the city.

Our belief system feeds and is fed by our conscience. When we are observing children at play, we usually see the beginnings of conscience as children start to be aware of the outcome and implications of their actions. Small children will check out whether we are frightened or hurt or cross. It is suggested that in certain personality disorders there is an absence of conscience, that the individual is unaware of the implications of his or her actions. We could also suggest that the internal states have become distorted and that one or more dominates the others.

Of course to a greater or lesser extent, our belief system influences all four states and affects them if, for example, we become disillusioned. Our disillusionment not only affects how we see ourselves but also how we see the world. When we are unwell, one aspect can dominate the others, and those who seek our assistance as clients usually have their vulnerable sides in control. They may also have become de-skilled or have lost their guide or artistry, or had their belief system shattered.

The task of the dramatherapist is to enable vulnerable people, as far as is possible, to restore their internal states to a balanced equilibrium.

This means that we address all aspects of the client rather than just the vulnerable side, which may be what is initially presented to us. Professional carers can sometimes see people as a collection of issues that need assistance rather than seeing the issues in context. Therefore to be able to work with people's strengths rather than just their perceived weaknesses is, in my view, a healthier way to approach therapeutic intervention. Dramatherapy admirably lends itself to this task so that the therapy becomes more a process of building on strengths rather than concentrating on vulnerabilities.

These general states are also more specific when we consider the dramatherapist. The skills are those of the trained dramatherapist, the guide is the internal supervisor, the artiste is the creative dramatic part of ourselves and the vulnerability is that aspect that can emphathize with clients. In terms of our practice, the vulnerability makes the connection with a client, the trained dramatherapist informs us how to work, the internal supervisor monitors this work, the artiste informs all the states in terms of it being creative, and our belief system ensures that we practise in an ethical way.

6. Ritualization of life events

Until recently, anthropologists have tended to refer to rituals as observable dramatic phenomena that exist in varied forms in all cultures. Dominant symbols are regarded as the smallest units of rituals and are irreducible. However, it is perhaps more useful to consider the process of **ritualization** in societies and cultures. We place a ritualistic frame around certain life events such as birth and death which enable a special form of re-working to take place which is both collective and in the public domain. We also ritualize aspects of our belief system in order to make symbolic statements which affirm our belief. All the arts are a part of ritual: art, music, dance and drama. Drama is also the means by which a ritual is performed. Rituals, like drama and theatre, are performed and involve the transition into dramatic reality from everyday experience and back again. We find rituals of health as well as rituals of healing, and the relationship between theatre and ritual could be one of degree rather than difference. One very important feature of ritualized events is that by and large we know what to expect. Our cultural rituals are familiar. So, for example, when we attend a naming ceremony or a funeral, we more or less know what to do and what our roles are, or there are people close by who will prompt us; weddings usually only have one rehearsal even for the main protagonists.

Dramatherapy sessions are ritualistic in their form and structure and usually start and end with familiar ritualized expression; this acts as a container for the exploration and risk taking within the session in which participants encounter material that is less familiar or unknown.

Figure 6.2 Some masks

7. Expansion of roles and transformation

Through dramatherapy it is possible to expand people's roles in relation to their world and to develop more flexibility and role choice. As we have already discussed, it is possible for people to become trapped in a closed role-system that can be very frightening to break. The repetitive cycles that I discussed under 're-working' can be moved on through an expansion of roles within the dramatic structure. And it requires a careful choice of dramatic themes and texts to facilitate this process, but it is possible to transform our experience of ourselves and others.

In the example of the dramatization of Jacob's ladder, the group could have created a simple narrative story. However, we used every dramatic device in order for people to enter the drama in a way of their choice; so they could be stones or pieces of a ladder and thus maximize their role expansion. A familiar almost ritualized story was taken and dramatized in new ways so that people could encounter themselves and others in the dramatic reality, in order to re-work repetitive patterns in their everyday reality. No-one was more surprised than the participants.

8. Lived metaphysical experience

There are many times when we feel touched by an experience, a vision, a sudden spectacle. Often this happens at the most unplanned moment, and anticipation is not always fulfilled. I remember a recent holiday in Eire when I parked the car near the water, determined to see the 'sun go down on Galway Bay'; imagine my chagrin when I woke up several hours later in the pitch dark with no itinerary. However, in our creative development it is possible to have special moments that catch us unawares and which push our dramatic borders further in order to move into the metaphysical. Epic scale theatre where the struggle of opposites take place through larger-than-life characters. How moving is the story of Odysseus when he encounters the one eyed giant, Cyclops whom he outwits by calling himself 'Nobody'. In these great stories we often find that it is the trickster character who enables us to find solutions rather than the hero characters. Tricksters are better at improvization whereas heroes often travel in straight lines, even though they do get lost.

We have focused on the important core concepts in dramatherapy: theatrical distance, everyday and dramatic reality, embodiment–projection–role, dramatic structure of the mind, re-working of experience, ritualization of life events, role expansion and transformation, and lived metaphysical experience. We have realized these concepts not merely as ideas, but from our own dramatic experience. In other words, we have encountered theatrical phenomenon and I would suggest that we have all been touched by it; perhaps not in ways that we would expect. But then that is the nature of theatre art and the creative process. It catches us unawares, and perhaps that is why it is so elusive. To define our dramatic experience is extremely difficult and at the end of the day we have actually to do it. This is why I suggest that the exercises are limiting in that they are, for the main part, projective exercises unless we have found a drama-partner. Nevertheless, maybe the gap in the theatrical curtain has been pulled back just enough to give us a glimpse, and that will be all that matters.

Exercises

Perhaps it is time to return to your own dramatized history and see how these concepts relate to the various events you have recorded. Maybe you wish to find another way of coding your record with colours or symbols in relation to this chapter. Be prepared for new events to occur to you.

Try to draw your own mind structure on a new piece of paper. Write or draw in the different segments your personal details concerning the four states and your belief system. Which of your states do you feel is the strongest? Is there one that needs particular attention at the moment? How has this structure been influenced by the previous information you have garnered on your roles?

Does your dramatic mind structure actually function in all its segments? Perhaps you would like to reflect on possible changes in your life patterns.

CHAPTER SEVEN

Dramatherapy in Practice
'Who holds the end of the thread?'

How is dramatherapy applied and with what types of populations? If I suggest that dramatherapy is appropriate with all populations, I might be accused of suggesting that it is a universal panacea. Dramatherapy should be flexible and adapted to the needs of the client group and the declared objectives for the dramatherapy work.

This chapter will look at the skills of the dramatherapist, and at how dramatherapy can be modified for different groups (and sometimes individuals). It will also consider suitable themes and texts for use in application. I trust that I have been able, in any case, to demonstrate that dramatherapy builds on the intrinsic and learnt processes that are part of our heritage. I am specifically addressing the dramatherapist or the person who aspires to be a dramatherapist, and from time to time will address this person as you, or the reader.

Some personal reflections

In your explorations it is important to consider what attracts you about theatre and therefore the subject of dramatherapy. Has theatre has always held a fascination for you? Maybe you have had a love–hate relationship with all things theatrical or perhaps there are unresolved issues about drama and performance that date back to negative situations at school. Some people suffer from being told that they are not artistic or that they are making a fool of themselves. Are you doing dramatherapy more for yourself or for your clients? Of course there will always be some resolution of your own themes, but it is important to be aware of them, as no doubt you have discovered through the various exercises and reflections.

*Figure 7.1 The Prodigal Son squanders his inheritance. A workshop on the
Prodigal Son with adults with severe learning disabilities in Germany*

Perhaps you perceive dramatherapy purely as a technical means of doing
therapy and that the artistic base is not the crucial element. If this is the case
then you will find much of what I am saying frustrating and at variance with
your own current thinking. I am not asking you to agree with me, merely to
look at things from other perspectives before making your own decisions
about the healing nature of theatre art, and therefore the principles and
practice of dramatherapy.

We shall also consider the needs of our clients and the best way to
facilitate dramatherapeutic work with them. The questionnaires about
ourselves will assist us with this task, and we can use them to create a client
questionnaire for use in the pre-group stages.

We also need to be aware of our own assumptions about client
populations which are often based on our view of whether people are like
ourselves or not. Our received perceptions about other people lie very deep
and are often rationalized rather than understood as prejudice. For example I
have been criticized for working with groups of people who have committed

Figure 7.2 From the Odyssey dramatherapy project at Broadmoor Hospital. The central motif is seen as the death of all sailors on Odysseus' journey. Within this circle we integrated both the journey and the homecoming, with the dead sailors, the tree of life and Odysseus and Telemachus reunited.

serious crimes: that somehow they do not 'deserve' dramatherapy (or anything else unless it is punishment) and that I should be using my skills with victims instead. I find this a worrying precept because it precludes any optimism about the propensity of human beings to change or, at the very least, to see the implications of what they have done.

I personally do not believe that there is such a thing as an evil person – whether adult or child – but I do believe that people are capable of evil actions. However, even our definition of an evil action can vary according to our belief system and cultural context. The source of so much religious conflict and, it would seem, political conflict too, is that adherence to certain belief systems is seen as synonymous with holding the moral high ground. I think it is more important for me as a dramatherapist to be able to present possible choices and outcomes before decisions are made, no matter who the client population might be. My understanding is that one of the main aims of dramatherapy is to present choices and implications of choices. Some of these choices may well have ethical and moral imperatives attached to them.

A supreme example of this, of course, is *Much Ado about Nothing* where the plot as such is relatively simple, but where there are very skilled portrayals of relationships and stereotyped assumptions. Most of the characters are involved in making decisions based on their accurate observations, or assumed accuracy. The people are challenged in terms of what they actually saw, and realize they had assumed knowledge rather than seeing the evidence.

As so often within Shakespeare's plays we get plays within plays and dramas within dramas; the crux is when the 'bad brother' gets the serving maid to dress up as her mistress and then protest her love to another, as she stands at the window at night. Eventually the outcome shows that even slander can be discovered and that 'bad brothers' get their just desserts but not before rumour and gossip and misinformation has taken its toll.

The discovery of the falsehoods was made by the comic buffoons who were responsible for the night guarding of the town. Shakespeare challenges our assumptions in many ways as most of his plays illustrate, that the person whom we would least expect to discover 'truth', because of our own prejudices, is the only person who is able to see the way through. As we recall, it was Bottom who had the amazing vision in *A Midsummer Night's Dream*, and Launce who did the 'sculpting' in *Two Gentlemen of Verona*.

The dramatherapist's knowledge base

Drama and theatre

Since I have argued that dramatherapy is based on theatre art, it will come as no surprise to the reader that I emphasize practical theatre as a major part of the dramatherapist's skills. However, the dramatherapist is not just making use of some drama techniques but needs a wide range of skills and processes that have been practised and refined.

The dramatherapist needs basic working experience of movement, dance and mime; voice – both speech and singing; improvization; character work in improvization and texts; play performance both as actor and director; stage management; lighting, costume and design; masks and other props; writing skills and play construction; budgeting and administration. A placement in a theatre as a student observer who can 'make themselves useful' together with classes in artistic skills and the craft of prop making would cover much of what I have described above. However, it is important to remember that you are developing the **processes** not just the techniques of theatre, and these will take time. You will notice that in developing the skills of creating something, whether a mask or an improvization, you are also engendering an artistic process.

You need to observe and understand the passage between the two realities that I have proposed – everyday reality and dramatic reality – and how going to a theatre performance structures this in an observable and comprehensible form. When people suggest that theatre should break down barriers between art and life I think this is a contradiction in terms. It is because theatre maintains these barriers that it is such a potent force, not just in therapy but for the survival of the human species.

> **Dramatherapists are applying their theatre skills and processes with people who are usually vulnerable and 'at-risk'. Advanced and long-term training and supervision is essential, in order to protect these populations, and dramatherapists have a responsibility to experience these same theatre processes for themselves.**

There was a term more frequently used, 'the good all-rounder', which contrasted with being 'the specialist'. This is most important for dramatherapists because they will need to draw on a wide range of skills and experience to maximize their effectiveness. I do not want to get drawn into the debate of whether dramatherapists should be good actors – they certainly need to be able to perform in a variety of roles, both roles in everyday life as well as dramatic roles. They need skills as theatre directors in order to shape a creative piece of dramatherapeutic performance, and stage management skills in terms of punctuality and overall management are probably the most useful practical skills of all! You need to be aware of roles that you find easier and those you find more difficult, which you will already have begin to discover in your dramatized history.

For the dramatherapist who comes from a background other than theatre, at the very least they need a thorough grounding in movement and voice and experience of theatre performance, as insider (acting) and outsider (director). It is also important that you explore your own preconceptions about 'luvvies' for example, and received stereotypes about actors and theatre in general. There are numerous basic books on theatre and theatre history, but more important you need to go to the theatre and start to look at the various complex elements that make up the total presentation.

I was very encouraged recently when a senior psychiatrist proposed that dramatherapy trainees should spend less time on psychology and more time on learning theatre directing. This same psychiatrist was answering student fears about the content of the Odyssey story being used as dramatherapeutic material with clients with mental health problems. The students, who were still struggling with the concept of dramatic distance, wanted to know whether the monstrous characters such as Hydra, would make clients more disturbed. The psychiatrist's response was to suggest that psychiatric institutions in themselves were monstrous and could swallow people up and spit them out again!

It is also essential that dramatherapists of all sorts go to the theatre as frequently as they can, but certainly not less than once a fortnight. This should include theatre performances of all kinds from big scale classical theatre to the smaller experimental fringe; studio performances; new play readings, poetry and prose recitals, theatre-in-education and so on. There is a plethora of opportunities that do not cost a lot of money that will continue to nurture your dramatic experience and expand your range of material and opportunities. Dramatherapists continue to need theatre experience however skilled they are. It is important that you see as much work in performance as you possibly can and you will find opportunities to see previews of plays, dress rehearsals and so on. Constantly you will be asking yourself:

- what is 'therapeutic' about this performance?
- what is the 'subtext' and is there an unspoken message?
- how is this theme(s) resolved?
- was there an implicit or explicit moral conclusion, and how was it communicated?
- were the actors able to give permission for certain actions that would be unacceptable in everyday life?
- did the playwright have a particular intention in writing this play and was it realized through the production?
- how far did the director put his or her own interpretation on the text?
- were you surprised by the actors' portrayal of the story that perhaps you already had your own ideas about?
- were the images and characters life-size or larger than life?

- what was the through-line of the narrative?
- how distanced was this material from your own experience or most people's experience of day-to-day life?
- how involved were you in the performance and was this a physical, emotional or intellectual process?
- were you drawn into the experience that was being enacted in the performance space or did you feel separate from it?
- was this separation a deliberate intention of the production, or did it not 'work' for you as an individual?
- did you identify with a certain character?
- how involved was the audience and how did they express this?
- did the technical side enhance the performance or get in the way of it?
- how many of the art forms were involved?
- was it a good play from the performers' point of view, the directors, the playwright's?
- how did the designer contribute to the piece?
- how challenged or empathic or angry or depressed did you feel?
- were those feelings a reaction to the content of the play or the fact that it was poorly performed or written or directed?
- did the play make you think in new ways about themes and relationships?
- how did the play enhance your understanding of people with whom you do dramatherapy?
- were you less fixed in a particular mind-set than you were before, and how was this achieved?
- what were the special moments, metaphors and images?
- overall would you call it an artistic experience or even an aesthetic experience and what does that mean for you?

You will already have asked yourself many of these questions in your own dramatized history and now you can relate them to a specific performance. I suggest you try and see a performance with others. In checking your own history, see if you can get a picture of how your own aesthetic sense has grown and developed. In extending your own experience it is important to try and do this with others and not just from your own perspective; perhaps you could form your own group of friends or colleagues who regularly go to the theatre, create workshops, read plays for yourselves, talk with actors and directors and technicians; and have time to debate and discuss the intrinsic therapeutic potential of these experiences. A word of caution!

Please do not go to see the play in order to discuss from just a particular psychological or psychoanalytic point of view; otherwise you will miss many opportunities. In other words, see the play through your wide-angle lens rather than your telescopic lens.

Allow yourself to take a broad sweep of a performance. Keep your antennae as open as possible so as not to limit your experience, so you will also try not to be biased by the theatre critics. If you disagree with a theatre critic think about why; what did you see in the performance that was different; what basis was the critic using to form his or her judgements?

The dramatherapist needs to be able to call upon any of these skills and processes as a part of their practice and needs to be able to select the most appropriate way forward. Knowledge and practical experience of theatre provides the working base of dramatherapy so that we need to constantly be involved in the theatre in one way or another. We should not as dramatherapists only make use of theatre for our therapeutic work, otherwise we could lose our objectivity, or be merely satisfying our own artistic needs. All dramatherapists need to have their own means of developing their artistry in a continuing and active way. To be involved in a continuing experimental theatre group is a very rewarding way of doing this.

Now the consumer

The client, or people with whom we work in dramatherapy, we hope will have a choice of whether or not they participate. I shall describe below the possibilities of open sessions for people before decisions are made concerning regular participation. However, whatever the information you may have about your clients, the most important source of information is the client. They will tell you what they think are the major life issues that need addressing and what they hope to get from your sessions. So often we rely on what everyone else says about them rather than trusting their own knowledge base, which of course feeds right into hierarchical relationships and power bases. Clients want to know where you are coming from and about your training and experience. This is a valid inquiry and forms part of the client's curiosity as well as illustrating their own feelings of self-preservation. I do not include the answering of personal questions within this frame, but it is important that your clients feel they can trust your integrity, that you have some idea of what you are doing, and that their expectations and your aims meet somewhere in the middle.

As well as your dramatherapy and theatre knowledge, and the client information that they have given you, you will also need to know about the clinical context within which your clients are placed, and the various theories that form the thinking of your non-dramatherapeutic colleagues. You need to know if the clients themselves are aware of the diagnosis and the aims of the treatment already in place.

It is obvious that you will need a thorough knowledge of diagnostic categories and how these are assessed and treated. Your professional team will usually consist of psychiatrists, psychologists and various therapists and you should understand their theoretical frameworks, their roles in the diagnostic and treatment processes, and your place in the multi-professional team.

Dramatherapists do not need psychological knowledge in order to make a psychological diagnosis but they do need to understand how other people think and how that thinking complements or differs from their own. It is important for dramatherapists to be able to collaborate and it is immediately beneficial for clients if they are within a collaborative rather than a competitive regime. It is sometimes a surprise to various clinicians that dramatherapist have evolved, and indeed are evolving further, their own research methodology and diagnostic observations; and indeed are able to take a dramatic history and dramatic state, just as clinicians will take a psychological profile and a mental state.

Culture and context

You will need to have a basic working knowledge of social anthropology both to understand people in their social and cultural contexts as well as a range of rituals, symbols and myths in their cultural context. Anthropological understanding will at least guard against our using a myth for example, purely from a psychoanalytic perspective or as a way of reinforcing this narrow view of human nature. I recommend that dramatherapy trainees conduct fieldwork in a different culture from their own, and that they have the opportunity for community placement as well as clinical.

Throughout this book I have emphasized the contextual importance of both the client and the dramatherapeutic material so that we do not assume explanations from our own limited viewpoint. It is important to consider whether certain rituals and stories are applicable cross-culturally and what meaning carries over into a new situation. How can we ensure respect for sacred stories that do not necessarily belong to our own sacred tradition without on the other hand, becoming eulogistic and reverential about all myths and legends, as if they hold the mystical key to all of life's happiness?

Keeping the balance

Perhaps what I am trying to say is that it is important to be able to have a balance in your dramatherapy practice and on the one hand be able to take people seriously and to have empathy and concern for their painful experiences, but on the other to encourage a sense of humour and some healthy irreverence. How does one gauge the sensibilities of the people in our groups, and would certain individuals be more relaxed if they could broaden their world view? Again, dramatherapy and theatre can allow people to explore views and ideas that are quite opposite from their own, through the safety of the distance.

Something a dramatherapist notes is when people tend to choose similar roles, whatever the story; for example when someone always chooses to be the good helper, the dramatherapist will find ways for roles to be expanded. This can be achieved through random role play – that is, the names of all the characters are put into a hat and each person chooses one. Another way is to find a text where there is a 'good carer' that is a many sided character, for example in Brecht's *The Good Person of Sezuan*, and I am sure you will think of many more instances.

Resources for dramatherapy work

It is a good idea to start your own dramatherapy resources folder where you keep ideas and thoughts, quotations and themes for possible use, and a little notebook where you can write things down when they occur to you – in the street or going for a walk. It becomes a veritable storehouse; but remember too that the people with whom you work will also have a storehouse or perhaps we should call it a storyhouse. People have very important memories of poems, songs, plays, books, as well as the personal events they will have recorded in their dramatized history, so find ways for them to be able to contribute to the creative process. It is perhaps more creative for clients to be invited to contribute a favourite fairy story than to talk about their various 'dysfunctions'. Psychotherapists are often unwilling to accept all material from us; it has to be certain sorts of material. As Martha Freud said in a recent play *Mrs Freud and Mrs Jung* about material:

> 'It was all about material; I always thought it was a strange word to use, as if it was something they cut off long rolls; make some nice cushion covers maybe, shape it, seam it – but in fact it was the opposite – it was pulling down the curtains...'

The integrated approach

You will be able to consider the parallel development of people when you place psychological development alongside dramatic development, as well as physical and social development. You will find that many plays are excellent to assist our understanding of pathology: various mental health states, dysfunctional families, and trauma of all kinds are richly portrayed, especially in texts and stories from Shakespeare and the ancient Greeks. Your knowledge base within the multi-professional team allows for an overall integration of world views where difference can be acknowledged as well as similarities understood. This has a healthy impact on clients where they can sense, even if they cannot articulate, divisions between staff members. And theatre itself is an integrative experience where feeling and thought come together.

The passionate performer

Having said all this in a rather dispassionate way about what you need to know in order to work with clients, let us remember that it is the capacity to feel passionately about people, especially the people with whom you work that is most important. If you feel passionately about people and life, then you are likely to feel passionate about the work you do, which will enable the creative potential to flourish both in your clients, yourself, and I hope, the institution.

**One of the greatest assets you can be to the people with whom
you work is to be to engender creative energy and artistic passion on their behalf, without superimposing your own view of
the world.**

Dramatherapists need to be permanently curious about the world and the
people in it and to understand how easy it is to get into a fixed view of the
nature of human beings. Clients are also helped through this curiosity which
isn't always concerned with the question 'why?' but rather keeps considering
the question 'how?' For example clients will often ask us why they are like
they are: 'Why am I like this?' they say and either we struggle to answer them
or else we look omniscient and reflect the question back to them, 'I wonder
why you are asking me that' and clients can feel de-skilled or even stupid.

The dramatherapy journey

If we consider the how of the experience rather than the why i.e. how did I
come to the place I am now; the present is immediately put into a context,
and the now can be seen in relation to the past and future. I do not mean a
single event in the past that is supposed to be the cause of all my troubles and
distress.

The how takes us into a journey where we can see the accumulation of
experience, the life journey with the misread signposts, the role expectations
that were impossible and the gaps in our own dramatized development that
would equip us for dealing with the vagaries of life. As we know, such life
journeys can be explored through dramatherapy, not in a direct way of 'This
is Your Life' but in a symbolic way through the means of the larger story: an
existing text or tale.

When people are lost on their life journey, surely they are helped by
providing a structure within which they can find new signposts, new
directions, movement and resolution. Great stories and plays already have
this structure and enable people to embark on a journey in a distanced form
which will paradoxically come close to their own experience. I keep referring
to Shakespeare but having used his texts in a very wide range of settings with
all type of populations, including groups from many different cultures, I am
even more convinced of Shakespeare the therapist!

Breadth of experience

Quite apart from your own dramatic experience and your curiosity about and passion for people, perhaps you need to consider your own breadth of experience. Do you have enough **breadth of experience of life** in many of its manifestations to be able to work with the complexities of clients? Perhaps as I suggested above, it is important to embark on some life journeys for yourself in order to encounter variations in life's pageant.

Material for dramatherapy use comes from many areas, the most important of course being the clients' lives; most of the techniques acquired through a drama training are important, and you will need to be conversant with a wide range of literature: plays (including Shakespeare, ancient Greeks), myths and stories, novels, poetry, films; the Old and New Testaments, The Koran and other major religious texts; as well as books about theatre processes (especially cross-cultural), including rituals of health and healing.

General principles

If you start from the basis of the EPR development with your client group (or individual) and take time for the processing of a pre-questionnaire before you start your dramatherapy work, you should avoid making the more obvious mistakes. Nevertheless, we all do it! I still recall with discomfort the off-beam mistakes I have made, for example underestimating a client's level of function or making assumptions about their personality or choosing quite inappropriate material.

It is your skill in facilitating, and drawing into a dramatic structure the themes and stories of your clients that will enable a creative episode to take place. You need to be aware that each and every session has its own structure that starts with the creative engagement of the group, develops a dramatic theme and then disengages and closes. This is the same for each and every group, whether there is a series of sessions, or just a number of single sessions. In a series, do not have too many in the first instance, before you do a joint evaluation with your clients. So a series of, say, six sessions, and then an evaluation and appraisal, is very helpful both for you and for your client groups. Before it starts, of course, you will have had your pre-sessions where you have been able to use a questionnaire and at least one practical session when your clients can actually experience the methods you use, and you can observe them actively engaged in the process.

Many of us start with very high ideals about closed groups and commitments for the life of a group and so on, but often the actual work reality takes over. Many clients for many reasons cannot undertake open-ended commitment and generally speaking I think it is putting additional stress onto them, especially in the private sector when there is also a financial commitment. Personally I have worked best for myself and my clients with the initial two months, that is eight sessions of the two plus six (i.e. two preliminary sessions and then a block of six). An agreement or contract needs to be negotiated for this, in terms of mutual responsibility, and respect for the people involved and the environment. Confidentiality needs to be addressed so that the group feels secure that they are not going to be gossiped about on the one hand and on the other that they are being treated with the full range of professional expertise – this will also mean sharing your knowledge with your supervisor, and at times with the team.

I find that clients generally have degrees of what it feels comfortable to disclose; some secrets feel so terrible that initially they swear you to secrecy but as a secret becomes less shocking to them, they feel differently about who knows. I personally think that confidentiality is a graded experience and that certain disclosures are possible with the client's full agreement. If we take confidentiality to such extremes we may unnecessarily mystify a process and even preclude healthy discourse within the client's own family for example. Generally speaking, I let the client set the guidelines unless there is a question of human safety or the breaking of the law. Then the dramatherapist will sometimes have to act on their own initiative but there is always the guidance from their supervisor as well as the codes of ethics and practice laid down by the professional association.

How long is a session? I find it curious that dramatherapists generally have adopted psychotherapeutic time structures of the 50 minute hour for individuals and one and a half hours for groups, usually on a weekly basis. I have not yet found the research to suggest that these are ideal times and in my own practice have experimented with others. Generally speaking, I think a session every two weeks is plenty of therapy for most people and in some of my groups they have been three or four weekly. Training groups I have also run on a six weekly or two month basis and found the learning curve both very intense but also very well assimilated.

My groups with offender patients I usually run on a three weekly structure with each group being three to four hours with a short break in the middle. I like to term these groups dramatherapy workshops rather than groups so that there is no confusion with the other groups that these clients may be experiencing. The longer exposure gives more satisfactory time for work to be developed and the gap in between allows for assimilation and preparation. I have also run groups for a full time week and recommend that as another alternative. Vulnerable people are not always helped by long term work as it is still keeping them away from their own autonomy and selfhood. It is very positive when clients are enabled to negotiate their own time frame and then have the opportunity to evaluate it.

Remember your own internal client, supervisor, dramatherapist and artiste and how they can all guide you in the dramatherapeutic work that you do. All those internal states are needed in order to keep a balance both for yourself and your clients. Do not neglect your internal artiste or you will find that your dramatherapy work becomes impoverished and you will begin to feel depleted. It is very easy for us to neglect our own creative sources.

Theatre is yours, to explore and challenge; guard it and contribute to it, and good luck on your dramatherapy journey. It will always be full of surprises.

Exercises

Write down a list of creative activities that help you expand your own 'internal artiste', and consider how frequently you do them. Do you allow yourself to be creative in all your rooms for living or are there divisions? Can you be creative at home as well as at work?

Perhaps now is the time to look back at all your answers and notes and start to regroup them in various ways. Perhaps you could colour code them. You could sort your experiences into Embodiment, Projection, Role headings and look at the dominance in any one of them – especially when it was influenced by others. For example you may find that there has been a predominance of E – physical games, dance, sports and so on; or a preoccupation with P – reading, writing, painting, model-building and much else; or have you had a dominance of R because you have been involved in drama in many forms or been conscious of 'performance' in your life and social roles. In general terms, most of us feel comfortable in one of the three states – or we discover that we are in one of the states but have always longed to be in another. How much is this influenced by others in your life? What is stopping you making that change?

Remember that theatre is about ritual and risk. On the one hand it gives us stability through ritualization of life events and on the other hand it encourages us to take risks. Consider the balance of ritual and risk in your own life.

CHAPTER EIGHT

A Biographical Muse
'Hanging by a thread'

This chapter is a personal reflection concerning my own dramatic development which seems to have gathered momentum as I approach 60 years of age. Since I think this will probably be the last book that I write with dramatherapy in the title, it seems right that I also put myself in the frame or on the stage.

I was a war baby, born at the end of 1938 to a dancer mother and doctor father, with one sister – the eldest – and then two brothers and then myself. As soon as war broke out, my father moved us out of London to a series of houses all over the country, where he was a locum for other doctors that had gone into war-service. My most vivid memories are of the house in Devon, at a tiny seaside town called Appledore where my father was not only the local GP but also the naval doctor for the warships that came and moored in the bay. My younger sister came towards the end of the war.

I went to dancing classes from the age of three, and of course with a dancing mother, received every encouragement. My embodiment was well and truly established. In addition, the fact that my father was a GP meant that we were surrounded as a family by patients and the healing professions. People might ring up at any time of the day or night or come and ring the door bell and expect to be seen. My mother, as well as running the local dancing school, acted as a receptionist for my father. Perhaps I need to say a little more about my parents.

My mother was Alice Edna Moynihan, and did not start to train as a dancer until her mid-teens; she danced professionally in the *Rosemarie* company and *Hassan* tour and set up her own dance school in London. While on tour she caught typhoid fever and was told it had left her with a weak heart and that she must never dance again. While moping around, a friend showed her an advertisement for a sculptor's model, to model a Canadian war memorial commissioned by the Canadian Government. This was to commemorate the Battle of Arras, at Vimy Ridge in Northern France where 60,000 Canadian soldiers had been killed. The sculptor, a Mr Allwood, lived in London. He met my mother, measured her shoulders, said they were broad enough to represent Mother Canada, and six years' work began. The statue bears a strong family resemblance and we were all very proud to hear that it had been unveiled in 1936 by Edward VIII in France.

My father was the second youngest of six brothers and sisters who had known my mother from teenhood. The families lived near each other, but it was not until their twenties that my parents knew they were in love and wanted to marry. My father had not yet finished his medical training, having failed his finals, and his mother cut off his allowance because he wanted to marry my mother. In the end they ran away to marry and told everyone afterwards – the families were furious. Dad continued with his medical studies, helped out by my mother who was still modelling the statue.

Two such people coming together certainly made for a curious family dynamic – mother, the most beautiful creative dancer, ever trying to be the good doctor's wife and my father a strange mix of tradition on the one hand – especially concerning women's roles – and unconventional and a pioneer on the other. He left the NHS very shortly after it came into being, because he did not agree with the bureaucracy and the erosion of his own freedom. From then on he ran a Robin Hood rural practice where the more wealthy farmers enabled him to continue to treat impoverished families, and a smallholding meant that we were able to have fresh dairy produce and eggs and mountains of apples and walnuts. My mother established a small local dancing school for young children and continued as my father's receptionist.

One very vivid memory is of the electricity being cut off because my father refused to pay the bill 'on demand'; all in his own good time was his motto and if he did not demand money from his patients, why should people demand money from him. He then had his own transformer installed so that the electricity board and himself did not need to cross paths or swords again!

There was no doubt that he was an excellent doctor, delighted in delivering babies, especially at home and would never hospitalize people unless it was essential. He refused to write out prescriptions for people but continued to do all his own dispensing as he had always done. He did not agree with writing the names of the drugs on the bottle because 'a little knowledge was a dangerous thing', yet he would go well beyond the call of duty in constant care for his patients. I recall his irritation when health and safety people said he had to make his surgery and drug cupboard more secure, and his smile of appreciation when patients would leave payment in kind on the back doorstep. My mother rang me up in tears once saying that a crate of cauliflowers had been left for them, and this was before freezers.

I spent most of my time wandering the fields and lanes, inventing my own adventures with some similarity to Arthur Ransome stories, finding out that a useful role within the family was that of entertainer, and also realizing that already I was an insomniac. Although I was meant to go to bed at the same time as my younger sister, I would creep out of bed and sit at the top of the stairs for several hours or else read under the bedclothes. I read everything from Enid Blyton to my father's medical text books, and the grown-up newspapers. The most important book that was given to me at this age, wasn't as you might expect, a book about theatre, but a book called *The Black Riders* by Violet Needham. I read this book so many times that I knew it by heart and loved the story of this boy the same age as myself who witnessed some freedom fighters and was therefore not allowed to return to his family but went with the fighters until captured by Count Jaspar. I shall return to this story later.

Having danced all the way through my childhood both at my mother's school and then at the local school, I assumed that that must be my career. My father's blind spot about women's roles seemed in particular to be about academic women and he did not encourage us to go to university. Thinking about it now, not going to university was not just for the daughters but also for the boys. None of us five children went to university in our teens or twenties and it was my older sister and I in our thirties that elected to go for degrees and higher degrees. My father was clear that women grew up to be wives and mothers and not to have careers. Somehow a career on the stage was all right because it was something one could do until marriage and then of course teach if one wished – just like my mother.

At the time this seemed the norm for all of us and it is only in looking back that there feels a strange mix of perverseness and eccentricity, innovation and tradition. Meanwhile I passed my eleven plus, got the highest mark in the country for the intelligence test, (my mother cajoled the information out of the headmistress of the two room village school where I went when I was eight). I went to Rugby High School for girls where I became the bane of most people's lives.

Just before I started secondary school, apart from the regular theatre visits to see the touring ballet companies, I had been taken to Stratford-upon-Avon to see *A Midsummer Night's Dream*, at what was then the Shakespeare Memorial Theatre and been absolutely transported. Whatever the future might hold in any direction, I knew that I had to go into the theatre, perhaps as a dancer, but who knows?

School was of the sporting side and an interminable correspondence started up between my father and the head mistress concerning whether or not I should play hockey. My father said it was unladylike and anyway with a professional dance career in view, it was dangerous for me to do it. Briz (Miss Briseldon) said that it was good for girls to be in team sports and everyone enjoyed it…and so on and so on. My father won in the end but rather than be allowed to study something different, I had to spend the double period of hockey walking round the playing field – what a waste, and what sweet revenge for the games teacher. My dancing did not make me good at gymnastics and I was passable at tennis and netball. Then the onset of extraordinarily heavy periods made my life a misery. This was when you just 'waited, to see if they would settle down'.

Both at junior and secondary school I started various sorts of clubs – girls clubs to avoid harassment by the boys, I Spy Groups, Cactus Collectors and so on. My Latin teacher did everything possible to encourage me to collect cactus plants so that it would encourage my Latin. The only subjects that I bothered with were those I could see would be useful (English, French, history) together with those that I found easy (domestic science, religious instruction). The geography of rivers and land masses I found boring, maths I just lost track of, and chemistry and biology I avoided until I realized that actually a dancer needed to know how their body worked.

The art teacher terrified me so much and put such a fear of putting brush to paper that I came out in a fever every time we had an art class. I eventually devised a solution for the sarcasm and ridicule. I learned to paint one tolerable picture with the help of one brother – it was rather striking really with a tree on a cliff-top and the waves beating against the rocks below. I learned to vary this picture for every art homework.

So any further projective development was stymied until much much later. I was still dancing three weeks out of every four and now going to voice classes.

I excelled in English, especially in imaginative story writing, literature and the study of Shakespeare. It was time for O levels and I decided that I could really do Latin if I put my mind to it, so taught myself from books in the library by going right back to the beginning. I passed English literature, English language, maths, history, French, Latin and music, getting high marks for English language and history. I turned a deaf ear to pleadings from the class teachers and headmistress, left school, made a bonfire of all my books and uniform and tried to decide what to do with my life.

In order to contribute some earnings I started working for my brother on the smallholding and doing some reception work for my father; I travelled several days a week for dance classes and speech and drama classes. Drama School as such was out as my father would not fill in a means test for a grant – he said it was an intrusion of his privacy – but between us we paid for my local classes. I spent every spare moment at Stratford and a year later went for my first audition for a tour of the George Formby Musical *Zip Goes a Million*, weekly touring for £6 per week and pay for your own digs.

This of course was the parental paradox – me leaving home at 17 and going on tour, with warnings from my mother about shops that looked liked chemists but were not real chemists! Yet at the same time there was the idea that it was just for a while and then I would 'settle down' (a favourite phrase in our family) and have a family. After this tour I went to live in my own attic flat (a bedsit) in Leamington Spa and looked around for more theatre work. Meanwhile the head psychiatrist in the local psychiatric hospital asked me if I would be interested in doing some drama on the ward. So still not past my eighteenth birthday I went to work as Nurse Jennings – an auxiliary nurse in order to do drama but also to do all the other things that auxiliaries had to do, such as hold patients down while they were being given electro-convulsive therapy. This sowed some seeds until the next theatre jobs came along as a dancer in revue, schools tours of Shakespeare where the director would change the parts over at a day's notice in order to keep us on our toes, rep theatre and more touring. This was all interspersed with working as a waitress, chambermaid, housekeeper, nurse, barmaid and farm-hand. I still lived on the doorstep of the theatre at Stratford and I fell in love with the actor Harry Andrews, who became my mentor and later patron of my drama school and very dear friend.

I wasn't making a lot of sense of my life at this time, the theatre jobs were intermittent and I did not feel that I was much good at them. Some of my fellow performers thought I was a snob and too big for my tap shoes – I still felt excruciatingly shy and quite unable to find a mode of communication with anyone.

I got married and had three children and attempted to continue the theatre career, with some difficulty, though I became a very good croupier at night. I was raising fee money to pay for more studies because again I was being asked to use drama in special situations and felt I needed a wider knowledge base.

I was now working in special schools and a psychiatric day centre, trying to formulate what on earth I was doing. My marriage was sliding down the slippery slope, and not long after taking a theatre group across the Berlin Wall, and working at the Bertold Brecht Theatre in the then East Germany and in a large hospital for people with severe mental handicaps called Wittekindshof in West Germany, I moved out of the family home with a toddler and two schoolage children. I was beginning to grasp something about dramatherapy but there were a lot of doors to knock on. There were very few clinicians or educationalists who were interested in new ideas in drama. Gordon Wiseman and I banded together and, being very inspired by the work of Peter Slade, founded the Remedial Drama Group and then the Remedial Drama Centre. There were others working in the field at the time – Veronica Sherborne, Dorothy Heathcote, Billie Lindqvist and we were all doing variations of the same thing – using drama and movement with vulnerable populations and trying to find a language with which to describe what we were doing.

The Remedial Drama Group toured all over the UK and went to Germany, Holland and Belgium, working directly with patient groups in hospitals, special schools and cerebral palsy centres. We ran training workshops at the same time for all types of staff including doctors and nurses, physiotherapists and occupational therapists, psychologists and ministers of religion. This was all during the 1960s, long before there was any idea of it being part of an institution.

By the early 1970s I was getting increasingly frustrated with all the psychological models being suggested for dramatherapy and other arts therapies so decided to take degree in social anthropology to try and create a frame for what I was doing. In the end the London School of Economics persuaded me to do a postgraduate diploma since I was a mature student, where I was immediately dubbed 'the dance lady'. I became so absorbed in the subject that I then decided to register for a doctorate and do research in Malaysia. After a lot of official and familial battles, the three children, my foster son and I went off to the tropical rain forest for nearly eighteen months.

What an experience! The trouble was that I could not get away from healing theatre – I had intended to study the Temiar people's children rearing and rituals. What I was grappling with was the dramatized play of children, and the enactment of rituals of preventative health and rituals of curative health.

It was obvious that my embeddedness in dramatic performance and healing was my destiny, whichever way I approached it all from. We all returned to the UK to start all over again it seemed, both shaken and stirred by our long journey. After several false starts and another failed marriage, we settled for a while in the Midlands. I was then asked to start a dramatherapy training in a college. It seemed the logical step, even though I was not too sure what I was talking about. The course started and from the word go there were challenges with the institution. They saw it as a clinical application of drama, parallel to the application of art, I saw it as a cultural variation of theatre art. At least social anthropology was taught on the course and I found a budget that would subsidize the students going on theatre trips to Stratford-upon-Avon. At the same time another college asked me to start a training programme there and this time it was within a department of drama and had much more understanding of the process of theatre. Initially I was commuting to St Albans for the first half of the week and to York for the second half, until the former demanded full-time loyalty and I was appointed to the first full-time lectureship in dramatherapy.

It was a strange feeling but a task had to be done, beset with challenges all along the way. The art therapists did not want dramatherapy at the college anyway so a lot of resentment and fighting for funds continued and I wondered what I was doing with my life. However, feelings of duty prevailed and I stayed there for nine years, the longest that I had stayed in any job anywhere. When eventually I left it was because there seemed irreconcilable differences about the future of dramatherapy training. I also had the idea of setting up a private dramatherapy institute to provide a longer-term training, and this started in the Offstage Theatre space, in North London in 1987 and continued until my retirement from the Institute of Dramatherapy in 1994 when it went to Roehampton Institute. I had proved the point that dramatherapy training could exist outside of a college institution, much to other people's chagrin. Every attempt was made to marginalize the training both from other colleges and from the British Association for Dramatherapists. It was ironic that they approved the training programme I had started in Greece in 1988 but withheld approval for the Institute's course for another five years. Meanwhile I was working in Greece, Norway, Denmark and Israel and can state unequivocally that my happiest time of all was working in Israel. Despite the difficulties that this country has, it seemed to welcome dramatherapy and me with large open arms and I have been working there ever since, both as a performer and on the training programme.

As soon as I left institutional life I was able to complete my doctorate on the research in Malaysia, even though again it was somewhat unconventional in approach. Many academics do not like cross disciplinary research and in some ways it was not anthropological enough for anthropologists and not theatrical enough for theatre practitioners! Although I have written several books, the Temiar book was until recently my favourite.

My restlessness took me to live in Stratford-on-Avon, the place of so many early happy memories, and as part of the dramatherapy training we inaugurated the Dramatherapy and Shakespeare Symposium. Actors from the RSC contributed to the discussion and debate and of course it was from the event that the RSC first became involved with taking productions into Broadmoor Hospital a place I was to later work at myself, using Shakespeare's *A Midsummer Night's Dream* and Homer's *Odyssey* with offender patients as direct dramatherapy. I also had my big scare with cancer and had to have two lumpectomies, radiotherapy and medication for five years. Each free year is a blessing.

While I was in Stratford I suddenly recalled the book I had read as an 11-year-old – *The Black Riders* – and knew that I had to read it again. It took me a whole year to track down a second-hand copy and I wondered whether it would be as I remembered it. And it was! The adventure was just as gripping now as then, despite my more sophisticated journey through Inspectors Wexford and Morse and Kinsey Malone.

It was several years later, when I had moved back to London – having sold my house in Stratford, and knowing that it was time really to become a hunter gatherer again instead of a settled cultivator – that I had this extraordinary waking dream while I was in Israel. I awoke with a big smile on my face saying a line from the book – 'He was the only one to look Count Jaspar in the face and say him nay'.

It became clear – I had been doing this all my life – looking the various personae of authoritarian Count Jaspars in the eye and being able to challenge them and say No! This realization was so freeing, even though it had taken me almost 50 years to reach it, and I felt years younger.

It has also been extremely important to me to become a grandmother. My grandchildren have contributed much of the material to this book, my granddaughter Sophie, and grandsons, Harry, George and Alfie.

Now I am an itinerant player; touring in plays, occasionally landing a TV spot, travelling overseas, and very occasionally doing some dramatherapy training.

If I look back at my own life in terms of my EPR development it is interesting how it has gone through several cycles. Embodiment throughout my life has been so important – most projective work was disastrous until I discovered the joy of writing. I seemed to move between these two modes of expression in my teens until my theatre work took me dominantly first into dance and then into drama. My roles in everyday life as well as my roles in theatre did not sit easily on my shoulders, and the dramatherapy became a variant that seemed to give me direction. In dramatherapy it has been again a lot of E work, a lot of writing and P work and, as dramatherapist, an experience of myself extending my roles rather then me as actor in other roles. This conflict became intolerable over the last five years and the bits and pieces of theatre and directing I was doing was just not enough. I do see myself retired as a clinician and would be very surprised if I practise dramatherapy again. Maybe this is also connected with my concerns about the direction that most therapies are taking at the moment. Theatre is at the core of my own healing experience. I have discovered this through finding out about theatre in other settings, whether preventative or curative, whether in theatre performance or ritual performance.

I return to my premise that drama is the basis of human development and perception; it forms the basis of how we perceive and communicate about the world in which we live. Probably it is biologically driven, but most certainly shaped by culture.

Understanding Count Jaspar has helped me to integrate my E P and R and life now is as good as it can be.

Caliban: Be not afeard; the isle is full of noises,
           Sounds, and sweet airs, that give delight and hurt not.
           Sometimes a thousand twangling instruments
           Will hum about mine ears; and sometimes voices
           That, if I then had wak'd after long sleep,
           Will make me sleep again; and then in dreaming,
           The clouds methought would open, and show riches
           Ready to drop upon me, that when I wak'd
           I cried to dream again.

                                   (*The Tempest* Act III, Scene 2, 136–144.)

Figure 8.1 The Canadian war memorial

Adult Questionnaire

Introduction

You can try this questionnaire for yourself (or Group) or use it as a basis for dramatherapy work with clients.

The first separation is between the EPR categories: embodiment–projection–role which will relate to your interests and hobbies, your work, and your creative management of your life. I am not asking questions concerning the more intimate areas of your life which I feel would be intrusive and inappropriate. However you may well decide to ask yourself further questions outside the remit of this particular questionnaire.

Make sure you have a notebook and some paper, felt pens and crayons and highlighter pens. Give yourself a fixed time, say 20 minutes for a section. Try not to attempt a marathon and do it all at once, but take short breaks, or go for a stroll or plan to do a section at a time. You may as you do it recall that you only briefly commented on the here and now in earlier questions. Remember you can doodle or sketch or write down phrases that seem appropriate or even invent words if it feels right.

For example:

One of my academic tutors pointed out to me some years ago that the word 'frogging' as a verb did not exist as in 'to frog' or, 'they all went out frogging'; I was describing the activities of the Malaysian tribe where I did my doctoral research and felt it was all right to describe their hunting activities of fishing and frogging! Beside, I liked the sound of the word; so permission to make up words or sounds or pictures if it conveys what you are trying to communicate, so feel free to make this up or to improvize whatever you feel is right at this moment, today! Making up of course is the very basis our creativity.

Drama Questionnaire for Here and Now (adults)

Embodiment:

1. Describe any of the following physical activities that you currently practice on a regular or intermittent basis – indicate how often and whether with others or on your own.

    (a) any form of sport including health classes at the gym
    (b) any movement or dance form
    (c) any relaxation or physical stress management.
    (d) walking for its own sake and not just to get somewhere.

2. Do you prefer to do any of the above on land or in the water, indoors or outdoors?

3. Do you watch sporting or any other physical activities on a regular basis, if so, describe what the enjoyment is for you?

4. If you won £200 and could only spend it in one of the following ways, describe how you would choose to spend it:

    (a) a meal for two at a very special restaurant with wines and any other gastronomic delights.
    (b) something very special to wear that was not just mundane replacements of utility clothes that had worn out.
    (c) 24 hours at a health farm with various physical therapies such as massage and aromatherapy.

5. You have been invited out for the evening and you know that the evening does not include a meal; you only have ten minutes so would you:

    (a) have a bath before you get ready or
    (b) have something to eat?

6. when you want to unwind and relax do you:

    (a) feed your body
    (b) pamper your body such as bathing with oils
    (c) exercise your body?

Projection:

7. Do you draw, paint or sketch on a regular basis? If so, please describe.

8. Do you spend any time on creative writing such as stories or poems?

9. How much time do you spend on reading and what sorts of books or articles?

10. Do you enjoy cooking and do you do it regularly?

11. Do you enjoy gardening and do you do it regularly?

12. Do you decorate or refurbish your house on a regular basis?

Role:

13. How many different roles to you play in your work setting? List and describe them briefly, (for example if you are a teacher then you have several roles in relation to pupils and colleagues).

14. How many different roles do you play in your family? (For example you might be a spouse, a parent, a hostess and so on – a role is not defined by the activity, such as cooking, but by the context of the activity so cooking could be to entertain, care for the family and so on.)

15. How many social role do you play? (You may be a member of various societies or interest groups.)

16. How many of your roles involve leadership and responsibility?

17. How many of your roles involve the care of other people?

18. How many of your roles have a strong creative component?

Dramatherapeutic Activities:

19. Think of all the bodily activities that you do not usually do and choose one to spend an hour or even an evening on; be careful not to choose something too strenuous if you do not normally do this exercise and if it is particularly taxing; take appropriate advice, especially if you are not necessarily fit.

You might for example choose to talk a long walk in your lunch hour or to join an introductory dance session or to go swimming after work. Whatever you choose to do, be aware of how you feel after the activity and describe it in detail in your record. Did you enjoy doing it rather than what you would usually have done? Is physical activity something that you usually enjoy and forget to make time for or is it something you do not really like?

20. Think about the projective activities mentioned above and choose one that you have never done before or have neglected. Again give yourself an hour or an evening and record how you feel afterwards and whether you enjoyed what you did. You may not have paints or clay but you do have the crayons and colours that you are already using; if you don't know where to start, do a large doodle and then colour it in. Remember no-one else is going to judge what you are doing so stay relaxed about it!

20. You may find it helpful to draw your own role chart. Although this connects with our role work, nevertheless it is a projective activity to write it all down. Take a large piece of paper and draw a circle in the middle which represent you, then for each of the main categories of role, draw a line off with another circle (such as work, family and so on); then draw further line and circles off each of the main categories, and label them with any sub-roles; there may be sub-sub-roles. For example under your social roles you could have a sub-role of organiser of the darts team, and it would be possible to have a sub-sub-role of health and safety responsibilities for the darts team.

When you have finished you will probably have a piece of paper that looks like an electrical circuit diagram. What roles are missing? For example 'alone' roles that are not in your social category? Find a way of including them on your chart. Then look at your chart in terms of which roles you play most frequently in your day to day life and mark them with a highlighter; what roles get neglected?

Are there roles that connect across grouping, for example are you involved socially at your place of work? Find a way of indicating this with connecting lines. Are there any roles that are neglected that you would like to spend more time in? As in questions 16 to 18, indicate with colours roles that have leadership and responsibility, roles that involve caring, roles that are highly creative. Is there a tendency for one type of role more than another?

21. From your role chart choose a role you would like to modify for an afternoon or evening and plan how it would be possible. For example you might want to take less responsibility at your children's playgroup and state that you are available one afternoon or you may want to feel you can contribute to the preparation of the rotas at work and so on. It does not have to be a huge change, just a small step to see how it feels, and record the experience.

22. Think of a role that is not on your role chart and find a way of having a chance to play it for a short time. It may be that you have never arranged the flowers at church (this is both a change of role and a new projective activity) and would like to do so or you want to know what it feels like not to answer the 'phone to your social network for an evening and so on. Make sure you look at the role and its relationships, not just the activity which you will be doing or not doing. Record how it feels to have experimented in this way.

✛   ✛   ✛

These first questions are all about our EPR activity in everyday life and how by having a dramatic perception of them we can experiment with change for ourselves, and perhaps modify things so that we enjoy more the things we want to do. The next questions are still about our everyday life and involve situations that can be termed dramatic even though they are woven into our day-to-day experience.

✛   ✛   ✛

23. Sit in a relaxed position and close your eyes if it feels comfortable. Think about your day or your week and recall an incident that needed telling to someone else; did you 'rework', i.e. keep repeating it to different people perhaps using different voices and gestures with each audience until it was no longer necessary to tell it? Write down the details of this drama and whether you still tell it or whether it is now laid to rest.

24. Are you someone who entertains others in the course of your everyday life, do you have good stories to tell or jokes to repeat? Briefly describe.

25. Do you enjoy gossip both the telling and the repeating of it? What topics or people do you usually gossip about? Briefly describe.

✛   ✛   ✛

Have these further questions yielded any more information that could go on your role chart? Include it before you move on; you may well be ready for a break now in any case. Leave any more answers until you have had a walk and a cup of coffee or at least a chance of a change of environment. (I am tempted to write down a stage direction – 'one hour later'.)

✛   ✛   ✛

We are now going to play with some more dramatherapy activities which may well give us information about our lives and intentions and take us further into an understanding of drama and dramatherapy.

26. Wherever you are sitting, group together a pile of small objects that are near to you: teaspoons, table mats, candle and matches, things out of your pockets or purse – coins, tickets and so on. Place on a table a sheet of the A3 paper that you have used for drawing and then sit comfortably and close your eyes. Try to shut off other thoughts and considerations and focus on the here and now. Think about your life as it is lived now; think about the shape of your life, the colour of it; visualize it as if it is a picture; it will usually contain significant people, not only things that are important to you, but also ideas and concepts; maybe your ambitions and so on; only spend a two or three minutes on this imaging before you open your eyes. Then use the objects you have gathered round you to create the image on the paper; group them in relation to each other, making a three dimensional picture of your life as you see it right now; it is rather like taking a snapshot. Don't agonize over it! These object pictures are very mobile and may be done again and again; try and stay with the first image that you have created.

These object pictures are what dramatherapists term sculpting and they come in many forms, such as using toy animals, the contents of the dolls house and so on; this is mini-sculpting. If the objects are even smaller – finger puppets, worry dolls – it is called micro-sculpting. Sculpts can be larger – using chairs or actual people – and are known as life-size sculpts; they can also be larger-than-life and even epic size.

✛   ✛   ✛

How does it feel to have your life laid out before you? Are there any surprises? Has anything been left out or are there things that you wish were not in there? Spend a few moments looking at the totality of your picture and record any thoughts and feelings in your note book. Then look at the picture again and decided to make a small change – nothing major; you may decide to take something out or put something in or move things closer together or further apart. Limit yourself to one small change, make it, and then look again at your picture as a whole. Write down about the change and whether it makes the difference you thought it might; what are the implications of this potential change, as there is always a knock-on effect. Put your note-book away and do something else and return to your sculpt in a day or so, and see how you feel about it then. Are you going to implement this change in your life? Or a version of it? How does it affect how you see your life now?

✛   ✛   ✛

Sculpting is probably the projective tool used most frequently by dramatherapists. It can be used diagnostically to plan a dramatherapy programme with clients and can also be part of the EPR process. For example, a sculpt can be created and then people are invited to tell a fairy story about the sculpt. The fairy story establishes the dramatic distance through which people can get a greater understanding of their sculpt rather than just talking about it.

✛   ✛   ✛

If you wish to try out the story idea, leave sculpting for a while and then create a new one using a different set of objects, with the title, 'my work now'. Once you have made the sculpt, think of an historical heroic story that this could be an illustration for, and write it down. Which role do you have in this story? Is this a familiar role and do you enjoy playing it?

✛   ✛   ✛

You will now see how there are endless possibilities for exploring our life dramas through the projective technique of sculpting and already how many variations there are in its application.

✤   ✤   ✤

Let us now look at a role exercise which illustrates the possibilities of identification through familiar roles and scenes. This will only 'work' if you watch television and regularly view one of the soaps. Next time you watch an episode, have your notebook with you and something to write with.

27. As you watch the soap of your choice try and get into a mode of 'active watching'; do you have expectations of this particular episode? What do you want to happen? Whose side are you on in the current disputes? Which particular characters do you feel drawn towards? Which scenes do you become drawn into? What is it about this soap rather than another that encourages you to watch on a regular basis? Are there special moments that you remember? Do you think it is close to real life? Is the writing well done? Are the actors convincing in their portrayal? Would you stay in to watch this soap or at least make sure that you record it?

    Think about what you have written down and reflect on the the way that soaps attempt to portray 'real life' or 'people we all know'. Perhaps in the dramatherapy frame, even though we may think that some of the events are somewhat fantastic, nevertheless we would probably think of soaps as the closest to our everyday experience; in other words we would call it 'underdistanced' from our own lives. Be aware of how much you feel you understand about yourself by watching a soap and whether it resonates or makes an impact on your life, your thoughts and feelings.

28. If you are a regular theatre goer, the next time you go to the theatre, try and choose a drama with a strong narrative, a clear plot and well developed characters. If it is in a different time and place, that will add to the distancing process. Have something to write with and ask yourself the following questions after the performance either immediately after the play or as soon as you get home.

Were you familiar with this play and did you have any expectations before you went to see it? Do you feel that the playwright's intentions were carried out? Were you aware of the director's influence on the play? What did you notice about the design? Where you convinced by the performances?

Did you feel drawn into this play and involved in what happened? Were there particular scenes that you were more connected with than others? Was there a particular character that you felt close to? Were there special moments in the play that you can recall?

How much were you aware of the technical side of the play? Did it get in the way of your enjoyment? How many of the art forms were involved in this production?

How challenged or angry or empathic or depressed did you feel? Were those feelings a reaction to the themes in the play? Did any of these feelings take you by surprise? Do you think that other members of the audience had similar experiences to yourself or was your an individual response?

What phrases or single words or expressions or images are you left with from this play? Have they stayed with you? Would you describe content of the play as distanced from your own experience?

How much to you now feel you were affected by the play compared with your feelings about the soap? Was the fact that it was live theatre contribute to this difference?

If you are unable to go to live theatre at present, try the above exercise with a television drama. Choose a single episode play that has a strong narrative, plot and characters. Make sure that it is not a police drama or a 'who dunnit'. You could also get a video as an alternative. If the play is a period piece, as with the live theatre, it will also help with the distancing from yourself.

Try and watch the play without distractions and interruptions and when it is finished, ask yourself as many of the questions as possible that are listed above for the live theatre performance.

Do you feel you have learned anything through these last two experiences – the soap and the drama? Has the nature of drama become more understandable to you? Is the dramatherapist's belief in the healing nature of theatre a clearer concept now?

29. How recently have you attended a religious ceremony of any kind? Were you central to that experience; i.e. did you have a central role? How important were the costumes and decorations? How familiar to most people was the ceremony; did most people know what to do? How meaningful do you think the ceremony was to the participants? How involved was everyone in the ceremony? Were some people more active in the ceremony than others? What did the audience do in relation to the ceremony? How many of the arts were involved in the ceremony? Was there a feeling that it 'went well'? Was that an artistic or a religious feeling or perhaps some other?

Write down any parallels you can see between the ceremony and the theatre visit you made as a member of the audience witnessing a play. There are certain elements that are the same but there will also be some important differences, particularly concerning overt control. Nevertheless look at the similarities in structure, time and space.

✛   ✛   ✛

It is important that you take time between all these questions and experiences and allow time for assimilation. Be guided by your own levels of exhaustion and try not to expend all your creative energy at once.

Perhaps now you need to take time to read through all your notes about your own dramatized present. What do you feel you have learned about drama and theatre and has it made you more aware of certain aspects of yourself? When you have thought about this, go back to your role chart and see whether you want to make any changes to it.

Now perhaps you can return to any other charts you created and see what the relationship is between them and your current role chart.

With the questionnaires you have already answered you now have a tremendous amount of material about your own dramatic past and present. This material looks at your own dramatic development throughout your life and relates it to the dramatic structures of the present.

It is helpful if you look at connections through your dramas between your past and your present. Are the gaps always the same or have there been major shifts in your adult life? Can you describe the events that have brought this about?

30. Having read all this information that you have written down and drawn, write a story starting 'Once upon a time...' which tells in the form of a mythic journey or a fairy tale the main elements of your own story. Make sure the story has a narrative and brings the journey to a resolution. Use crayons to create pictures to illustrate your story. Let it come to rest after the expenditure of all this energy on your dramatic life.

+ + +

I have endeavoured to relate drama processes to your everyday life and looked at the impact of dramatherapy concepts on your life now. There have been some brief illustrations of how you might explore your current life through dramatherapy.

Much of what you have done has been projective in terms of it being recorded and written down, which in itself is a projective exercise. There have been various tasks for you to try out and then write down any possible changes.

The most important factor that is missing is that dramatherapy needs to be done with other people. You have in the main had an isolated experience, with this book being an intermediary between yourself and myself. Although, as we have said all the way through, that drama, theatre and dramatherapy need other people in order for it to be most effective, nevertheless you have had an opportunity to test and try it out for yourself.

If you do not already belong to a drama group, perhaps now is the time to explore that possibility more fully. Meanwhile I hope there have been some useful pointers in your current life journey.

Recording a Dramatic History

Exercises and ideas in practice

This section suggests how you can retrieve and record dramatic experience. If you are going to answer some of the questions, think of doing it with someone else. Drama is a social activity and needs the presence of at least one other person, but preferably a small group who are willing to do the exercises. If you have one other person then choose someone that you trust and that you share some mutual sympathy towards. Even if the other person, or your Ariadne is not going to do the exercises, make sure they have time and patience to help you process your replies without making any interpretations. It is the sharing of the dramas that is important not the explaining of them. Whatever you decide, remind yourself that you have your own internal Ariadne who acts as your guide. Either decide to complete the whole of the questionnaire after you have read the guidelines, or else choose one section to complete. Whichever you decide, the experience will give you a lot of information for your own inquiry into drama and theatre and therefore dramatherapy.

You may feel that you have no experience of drama or that it is something you are not good at or would not even like to be seen doing. Try and put your assumptions and any prejudices on one side; there will be opportunities to record them under certain of the headings. All I am sure of is that you will discover that you know far more about drama than you think you do and that you will have both been a participator as well as a director of many dramatic scenes. As I have suggested, it is for you to discover your own **dramatic development** with help of a few signposts.

We could either start from now and go back, or we can we scroll back to your earliest memory and start from there. I am going to start from now and go back to some of your earliest memories. You may not wish to complete all the sections at once but may prefer to complete a section at a time. This is your choice, but remember we are not writing long answers to all the sections. At most they are brief notes, phrases, squiggles and so on. When you have completed it, there may be sections you wish to go back to and write at length about, or illustrate with pictures or cut outs.

Of course you need to have something with which to write. I suggest a large exercise book that has both lined and blank pages, a packet of coloured felt pens, a packet of wax crayons and several lead pencils and a pencil sharpener. Lined and blank pages are useful because at times you may wish to write and at others you may find it more appropriate to draw.

I am suggesting that you use these materials in order to record your own dramatic diary – it will be a history that includes your experience from the present back to the distant past. You may well remember things that have lain dormant for a long time or things that fill out a previously puzzling picture. You may suddenly see a different perspective on something or recall a different version of a story that you had been told by someone else. This is because you are not just recalling your own narrative story, **you are recalling your own narrative drama in which you were often a participant or audience or director.**

If for any reason some of these memories distress you, put them alongside those that you enjoy and together see them as the ebb and flow of your life. We are not going to explain or analyze or interpret these dramas, rather we are going to record them. You will then have some understanding of your own healing dramas and be able to generalize into your understanding of dramatherapy and theatre of healing. I have suggested you choose someone to accompany you on this journey – either completing the questions too or discussing your feedback. You may decide to let your co-dramatist ask you the questions and you respond. Discuss with this person the possibility of setting up a role play when it comes to questions about roles.

Before you start to complete the questionnaire, consider the following points carefully and they will ease your journey through.

- give yourself a time-scale for the whole questionnaire (not more than two hours) or for a section at a time (not more than 20 minutes).

- follow the questions and notes sequentially because they have their developmental progression, and try not to gloss over sections in order to get to the end. This is not a test!

- try to record memories that are both positive and negative as suggested in the first few questions.

- a reminder not to try and write too much; these are impressions and quick notes and you can go back later to write in more detail if you want to.

Recording the Dramatic History

Before you start responding to the questions under each of the following age stages, take a few moment to concentrate on each period of time; imagine familiar land-marks such as the house/flat you were living in, your favourite room, people that were around, pets and special possessions.

There are useful words to prompt yourself with – who, what, where, when, why for example: who was there? What was happening? Where did it occur? When did it take place? (When in terms of precise time of month/year; seasonal time, morning/afternoon/night and so on.) Why was it happening?

Although many of the questions may be answered with words, phrases or sentences, you may want to sketch or doodle, you may remember a snatch of a song or an image that better records your experience. Record in as many ways as you wish.

Your current experience – now!

1. Write down as many words as you can, that relate to your experience of the words DRAMA and THEATRE. (Give yourself three minutes for this.)

2. Underline with a colour those words that have a negative feel about them, and use another colour to underline those words that have a positive feel.

3. Count up how many positives and how many negatives and write the two number in the right hand margin (eg 5n, 6p).

The next sections refer to questions about the dramas in your past rather than your present. Whatever your age now, make sure you respond to stages in the past.

Young adulthood (18–25 years) or adulthood (26 years plus)

4. Write down any experience of being in a drama group/class. Describe the activities and whether it was a positive or negative experience.

5. Describe any particular experiences of going to a live theatre, and any 'special moments' that you can recall from specific plays.

6. Describe any particular experience of going to live theatre that was a negative experience.

7. Can you recall in your adult life, any other experiences that could be called 'drama'? Having to do 'role-plays'? Getting up to speak infront of an audience? Please describe and comment on whether they were positive or negative.

Teens (12–17 years)

8. Did you 'do' drama at school? Describe whether you did it as a subject or as part of English or as an end of term activity or as an option. Describe the activities and performances/projects that you were involved in and whether they were positive and/or negative.

9. Did you attend drama classes outside of school? If you did, please describe.

10. Did you go to the live theatre? Describe any special moments or any experiences that were negative.

Young times (7–11 years)

11. Did you belong to a drama club or class? Describe what you did and what you thought about it.

12. Were you taken to the live theatre perhaps for a seasonal or birthday treat? Describe what you can remember and what you thought about it.

✛   ✛   ✛

The above 12 questions concern what we generally think of as drama and theatre and although we may have been taken to see a pantomime or been in the nativity play at a younger age (if so, please write down about the experience), we do not think about drama experience as beginning until at least seven years old. We may however use the term play instead of drama for earlier activities. You may also have memories of other people's attitudes towards these activities; maybe it was 'in' to be in the drama group or maybe it was the opposite; maybe your family did not approve of your doing drama (did you have to study more seriously?) Can you recall gender- ized attitudes towards dramatic activities that you have engaged in; for example were you encouraged to only take very 'feminine' or 'masculine' roles?

Having thought about these questions and recorded your answers, there are now some additional questions that are also to do with drama that perhaps did not occur to you as part of your dramatic development.

Return to the age stages above and answer the following for each stage. Again, take time to make the transition between the stages as you remember yourself at those times. On the other hand you may wish just to take one stage and answer all the questions around that stage. Be sure to tell your co-dramatist what you intend to do and make sure you still have enough materials to answer the questions in whatever way feels appropriate. Some of the sections may well be enhanced if you have access to photographs. Finally don't agonise over these answers and if a memory does not come easily then just move on. You will find that some answers will come when we are not thinking too hard.

✛   ✛   ✛

13. Can you recall celebrations for births, naming, coming of age, marriages and deaths? Were you a spectator or did you have a special role to play? Or to put it another way, did you have a peripheral or a central role in this special event? Please describe.

14. Describe any important bits of dreams and/or nightmares that you can recall at these stages? Were you playing a part in the dreams or were you the audience?

15. Write down times when you recall having imaginary conversations in your head or out loud? Did you answer yourself? Did you rehearse important events such as interviews in advance?

(If any memories start to flood back, just jot them down one-at-a-time with key words).

16. Describe your favourite daydream(s) and the role that you create for yourself in the daydream.

17. Are there important people in your life that perhaps are away from home or that have died, with whom you have had or are having private conversations?

(Some of the following questions you may like to enact or role-play with your co-dramatist, or perhaps use the appropriate voice and gesture.)

18. Do you enjoy telling stories about events that have happened in your present or past life? Do you just tell the facts or do you also use special voices, pauses for effect and dramatic punch lines?

19. Do you ever pretend to be someone else when you answer the telephone or when you open the door or make complaints?

20. Do you invent influential relatives or friends who will support you when in trouble? Do you ever create a family for yourself that is very different from the one you have?

✛   ✛   ✛

Most of us engage in these acts of drama during most of our lives, although we may not always think of them as drama; but they all involve playing a part or observing a scene, all in the reality of the dramatic imagination. They include scenes and role-plays and rituals of life events.

All that you have written down so far has been between the ages of seven years and your present age. You may also have sketched or doodled or drawn an image as part of your recall. We are now going to consider earlier ages and stages, which for some people may be more difficult to recall. Other members of the family may be able to prompt you or you can find that, by not trying too hard, the memory will return. Your co-dramatist may also be able to prompt you by asking indirect questions.

Childhood (4–7 years)

As before, you may need to spend a few moments recalling any special landmarks, especially as our memory can get hazier the further we go back; perhaps there were some significant spaces, hidey holes, clothes and so on that may help you recreate this earlier time in your life.

21. Describe any playground games that you used to enjoy playing and mention those that you did not enjoy but maybe were expected to play.

22. Write down any stories that you like to hear over and over again and whether you enjoyed enacting these stories. What character did you imagine yourself to be while listening or enacting?

23. Describe any imaginary friends you had and the sorts of conversations you would have to each other. Did you have adventures together? Any other activities you would do together?

24. Describe (or draw) any special toys that were like your personal friends or companions. Did they have names? What scenes would you play out together?

25. Were the 'dramas' you enacted under questions 23 and 24 private dramas? Were you ever stopped by an adult from having these scenes?

26. Describe your favourite play activities at this age and whether you played with others or on your own. Did you have special scenes that you enjoyed repeating? Special rhymes that you liked to hear again?

27. When did adults or older children join in play and games with you and when did you play with other young children or on your own?

28. Can you recall adults playing parts in the dramas with you or were they the story teller or did you 'perform' for them?

29. Did you experience childhood fears of any kind? For example recurring nightmares? Monsters under the bed? Spooky sounds in the cistern?

30. Did you have a magic place that you went to in your imagination, or a special place where you could hide and imagine it to be somewhere magic?

+   +   +

You have already done a lot of writing and recording, maybe you need some breaks and to continue this later. Again, leave time to do some processing with your co-dramatist or group.

Infancy (0–3 years)

This next stage will be to see what you can remember from even earlier in your life, or to find others to help prompt you. Record any memories however fleeting, especially any sensations: that is taste, smell, touch, sight and hearing.

31. Do you recall any special toy or possession? Did it have a name? Describe and draw what you can remember.

32. Do you remember talking to this special toy and answering **as if** you were the toy?

33. What sensory experience can you recall about this toy? (small, taste, sound, touch, sight).

34. Can you recall any singing games at this time?

35. Can you recall any stories or rhymes?

36. Do you remember drawing or painting or crayoning?

37. Do you remember playing with clay or similar substance? What did it feel like and what did you make?

38. Describe any other toys or sets of toys that you played with at this time. Did you tell stories with them?

39. Do you remember anything about the clothes you wore? Colours? Texture? Smell?

40. What can you remember about food? Favourite food? Its texture?

41. Can you recall anything about water such as playing or bathtime?

42. What physical movements can you remember such as rocking or clapping?

43. What physical movements can you remember that were shared with an adult? Who usually instigated the movements?

44. Can you recall adults selecting toys and activities on your behalf?

45. Can you recall adults censoring any of your playing activities?

✛   ✛   ✛

You have just written up a very detailed history of your own dramatic development. Some parts will contain more information than others and there will be stages that are very clear to you and others that have a vague outline. After this exercise you may find that other information occurs to you at a later stage or that information from one stage will feed into another. You may well find that there are drama experiences that have not been suggested here. Use the exercise book to record all these memories. Your co-dramatist or group members will also assist you to process your answers and help you discover new examples of your dramatic heritage.

✛   ✛   ✛

The first thing we learn by doing these exercises is that from a very early age we have done a lot of drama; we have exercised out dramatic imaginations from as young as a year old. We may find that some of the early experience is mimicry of an adult or older sibling, but we also find that we instigate imaginary tasks and actions. For example a colander is chosen as a hat rather than something from the dressing up clothes; indeed the contents of the kitchen cupboard usually makes far more exciting playtime than ready made designer toys. By talking to our special toy and answering as if we were the toy, we show that we are playing roles and entering dramatic action from as early as two years old.

We are also learning how much of what we played at was censored or selected by adults; playing can be gender specific with a particular choice of toy or can be dismissed as silly or a waste of time or not as good as your sister.

We can recall which of the playing experiences were pleasurable and which were private and which were public. When you have completed your history, see if similar patterns have always run through your dramas.

It is now time to start to group the different types of dramas that you have engaged in throughout your life. Remind yourself of the embodiment–projection–role (EPR) categories described below and use them to differentiate your experiences.

Our earliest experiences are usually physical and sensory; we play through the body and through all our senses and much of our body experience is with the close proximity of the adult who cares for us. Much of the information in this earliest part of our life will have to come from others, maybe there are family photographs that can assist us too. Since for the most part our mothers are our first carers, I shall continue to use the term mother in a generic sense.

Mothers will cradle and rock us and encourage us to co-operate with them in physical rhythmic experiences. They will respond to our singing and gurgling and sing for us. They will mimic us just as we mimic them. These experiences are most concentrated during the first year of life and are known as the **embodiment stage of our dramatic development or physical play (E)**. As we grow older we may still retain a lot of embodied experience especially if we play sports or dance, for example.

As we put our energy and attention into media outside ourselves, such as drawing and toy play, others around us will encourage and praise what we do: the first drawing of a person or making our letters or building a construction. We also enjoy others building while we knock it down. This stage of playing is called **projective play (P)** and as we progress it gets more complex. There are constructions we like to make on our own and those we like to share with others. All media outside ourselves with which we create comes within the field of projective play or projective creation. Although some people may continue to create in a projective way throughout their lives, when young they will still go through a stage which involves the dramatizing of roles.

We notice that children start to enact stories rather than telling them through the toys or puppets. Children put on voices and use gestures in projective play and use soft toys or puppets or the doll's house as a medium through which to project a story. As they start to enact roles themselves they are beginning to explore the stage of **dramatic play or role (R)**.

Quite apart from the specific answers you have given to the questions, you will also start to think about your own life now and how much you tend to focus in one direction or another. If it feels right that is fine, but you can always check whether you would rather be painting than jogging, or making speeches rather than writing them.

Using these questionnaires in practice

Dramatherapists and other workers in the field can use these questionnaires to assess people in their groups before they start their dramatherapy. They will get some idea of where the gaps are and perhaps some understanding of diagnostic categories that would be useful in planning the work. Just as other clinicians will take a psychological profile of a person, you can take a dramatic profile. Remember that if you are assessing, you can encourage your clients to be interactive in their answers through movement, sculpting and enactment.

This progression can be the same for the audience or for the performer and can be a way of structuring our dramatherapy and therapeutic theatre. This process needs more time that the conventional therapeutic hour or hour and a half, which is why most of my work needs three or so hours. Words like awakening, challenge, surprise, revolution, revelation and strength, occur to me as I write this description of theatre. They are all words that have a place in a dramatherapy storehouse.

Living Theatre Exercises

You have already written down words associated with your experience of theatre. Please add to this list any words from the questionnaires or from areas of theatre space or from roles and functions of the people who work there, that seemed significant to you. You may find there are phrases which occur to you that link with your dramatized history, such as 'I was always in the spotlight', 'I could never remember my lines', 'I never took off my mask'. You will start to associate scenes in your life with being the performer or the director or the prompter or the audience. What is the first recollection that you have of being able to influence the design of your life? Think about dramas that have been packed away and not recycled in your present life.

You now have some practical tasks to take this process a step further. They will both require larger pieces of paper, at least A3 size, pencils, crayons and felt pens. If you do not wish to do this exercise, just mark it as you read through with your own recollections. You may think about how you could apply it with your clients.

Exercise 1: Ground plan of a theatre

Take one of the large pieces of paper and draw a ground plan of a theatre for yourself. The descriptions of theatre spaces in Chapter Three can act as a prompter, so you can create a ground plan that feels right for you and your dramatized history. Some space may be bigger than others so you might have a small stage and a very big storage area, or the boundaries between the different areas may be less defined than in a most theatres. Try not to be too logical but use the theatre metaphor as a way of structuring your memories of your past life in a different way.

Note down dramas from your life that you feel were more important than others. Where are these located in your ground plan: the rehearsal room? At the stage door? Use crayons to colour significant areas including those affected by the mood of different lights. At the moment we are considering your past dramatized history, not your current life. On the ground plan, do the areas you have highlighted coincide with the observations you made in the questionnaire, in terms of clusters and patterns? There are no idealized pictures that are 'right', there are merely ways of experiencing things and alerting you to potential change and choice through new understanding – understanding through theatre.

Exercise 2: Roles and functions

On a second piece of paper, look at the various roles that belong to the spaces that you have now drawn. The question is, who functioned in your past theatre and what did they do? During our early life there will be a series of roles that are taken on by others and some might be combined. For example we may feel that our parents shared the directing and stage management between them and it was grandma who was the financial administrator. Draw a series of circles around a central circle that represents you and **write down their function in relation to a theatre role**. You can also indicate the relationship between these roles, whether they changed, and how skilled people were in them. You may want to indicate more about these roles through the use of colour. Try to keep it within the metaphor of theatre.

Exercise 3: Your own theatre roles

In the above diagram you drew a circle to represent yourself in the middle of the other circles which represented others. Now take another piece of paper and draw larger circle. You are still going to focus on your past dramas but now to concentrate on the various roles that you yourself played. You could represent these by drawing circles within the big circle. Try not to draw any roles in isolation but in relation to the spaces that you created on your ground plan. Again the roles can be coloured and give some indication of those roles that dominate more strongly than others. Did you duplicate or imitate roles that were also taken by people around you? Were there ones that were more successful than others? As you progressed through your life until now, did any of the roles change substantially? Are there roles that you wish you could change or modify or just give up? Do you want to maintain the wardrobe of others for the rest of your life?

You now have three pieces of paper which together illustrate your own theatre history on a ground plan and on two role plans. Place them side by side and consider yourself in the total context of what you have recorded. Be aware of the various colours on the different sheets and the progression through to adulthood.

What play is being enacted in this theatre? From all the various smaller dramas that you have recorded, what is the bigger story that took place? What is its title? It may be one you make up or the title of an existing play or novel or film.

Is this same drama continuing or are the changes that you hoped would happen now falling into place?

Finally, what play or what story does your life remind you of? A Shakespeare Comedy? A Greek Tragedy? A Contemporary Political Play? Find time to re-read the play or story or ideally see the play and reflect again on what you have written down.

Later on, take your own life-theatre into a bigger theme, and make it a part of the great story. Perhaps the big story will give you new possibilities and choices. You may have pictures and images and poems that will elaborate your story.

Bibliography

Artaud, A. (1958) *The Theatre and Its Double.* (Translated by Corti, 1977). London: John Calder.

Bachelard, G. (1942) *Water and Dreams.* Dallas: Pegasus.

Bachelard, G. (1964) *The Poetics of Space.* Boston: Beacon Press.

Barker, C. (1978) *Theatre Games.* London: Methuen.

Brinton Perera, S. (1981) *Descent to the Goddess.* Toronto: Inner City Books.

Brook, P. (1986) *The Empty Space.* Harmondsworth: Penguin Books.

Cambell, J. (1977) *The Hero with a Thousand Faces.* New York: Bollingen.

Cattanach, A. (1993) *Play Therapy with Abused Children.* London: Jessica Kingsley.

Cattanach, A. (1994) *Play Therapy: Where the Sky Meets the Underworld.* London: Jessica Kingsley.

Cattanach, A. (1997) *Children's Stories in Play Therapy.* London: Jessica Kingsley.

Cook, R. (1974) *The Tree of Life.* London: Thames and Hudson.

Courtney, R. (1988) *Re-Cognizing Richard Courtney.* (Edited by D Booth and A Martin–Smith). Ontario: Pembroke Publishers/Jessica Kingsley.

Cox, M. (1978) *Structuring the Therapeutic Process: Compromise with Chaos: The Therapist's Response to the Individual and the Group,* Reprinted 1988. London: Jessica Kingsley.

Cox, M. (1978) *Coding the Therapeutic Process: Emblems of Encounter: A Manual for Counsellors and Therapists,* Reprinted 1988. London: Jessica Kingsley.

Cox, M. (1992) *Shakespeare Comes to Broadmoor: 'The Actors are Come Hither': The Performance of Tragedy in a Secure Psychiatric Hospital.* London: Jessica Kingsley.

Cox, M. and Theilgaard, A. (1994) *Shakespeare as Prompter: The Amending Imagination and the Therapeutic Process.* London: Jessica Kingsley.

Cox, M. and Cordess, C. (1996) *Forensic Psychotherapy: Crime, Psychodynamics and the Offender Patient.* London: Jessica Kingsley.

Cox, M. (in preparation) *Remorse and Reparation.* London: Jessica Kingsley.

Dokter, D. (1994) *Arts Therapies and Clients with Eating Disorders: Fragile Board.* London: Jessica Kingsley.

Duggan, M. and Grainger, R. (1997) *Imagination, Identification and Catharsis in Theatre and Therapy.* London: Jessica Kingsley

Duvignaud, J. (1972) *The Sociology of Art.* London: Paladin.

Emunah, R. (1994) *Acting for Real.* New York: Brunner/Mazel.

Gersie, A. and King, N. (1990) *Storymaking in Education and Therapy.* London: Jessica Kingsley.

Gersie, A. (1991) *Storymaking in Bereavement*. London: Jessica Kingsley.

Gersie, A. (1992) *Earth Tales*. London: Green Press.

Gersie, A. (ed) (1996) *Dramatic Approaches to Brief Therapy*. London: Jessica Kingsley.

Gersie, A. (1997) *Reflections on Therapeutic Storymaking: The Use of Stories in Groups*. London: Jessica Kingsley.

Goffman, E. (1961) *Asylums: Essays on the Social Situation of Mental Patients and Other Inmates*. New York: Anchor Books/Doubleday.

Goffman, E. (1969) *The Presentation of Self in Everyday Life*. Harmondsworth: Penguin.

Grainger, R. (1990) *Drama and Healing*. London: Jessica Kingsley.

Grotowski, J. (1968) *Towards a Poor Theatre*. London: Eyre Methuen.

Harris Smith, S. (1984) *Masks in Modern Drama*. University of California Press.

Hellman, C. (1991) *Body Myths*. London: Chatto and Windus.

Hickson, A. (1996) *Creative Action Methods in Groupwork*. Bicester: Winslow Press.

Hillman, J. (1983) *Healing Fiction*. New York: Station Hill.

Hillman, J. (1992) *We've Had A Hundred Years of Psychotherapy*. New York: Harper Collins.

Hobson, R. (1985) *Forms of Feeling: The Heart of Psychotherapy*. London: Tavistock.

Hollinghurst, H. (1973) *Gods and Heroes of Ancient Greece*. London: Heinemann Educational.

Huizinga, J. (1955) *Homo Ludens*. Boston: Beacon.

Jenkyns, M. (1996) *The Play's The Thing; Exploring Text in Drama and Therapy*. London: Routledge.

Jennings, S. (1975) 'The Importance of the body in non-verbal methods of therapy.' In S. Jennings (ed) *Creative Therapy*. Banbury: KemblePress.

Jennings, S. (1977) 'Dramatherapy: the anomalous profession.' *Journal of Dramatherapy 4*.

Jennings, S. (1979) 'Ritual and the learning process.' *Journal of Dramatherapy 13*, 4.

Jennings, S. (1983a) 'Rites of Healing', paper presented to Dramatherapy Conference, London.

Jennings, S. (1983b) 'The importance of social anthropology for therapists', talk given to Royal Anthropological Institute, London.

Jennings, S. (1985a) 'Temiar dance and the maintenance of order.' In P. Spencer (ed) *Society and the Dance*. Cambridge: Cambridge University Press.

Jennings, S. (1985b) 'The Drama and the Ritual, with Reference to Group Analysis', paper presented to Spring Seminar Group Analytic Society.

Jennings, S. (1986a) *Creative Drama and Groupwork*. Bicester: Winslow Press.

Jennings, S. (1986b) 'Playing with ideas of play', paper presented to Art Therapy and Dramatherapy Summer School, St Albans.

Jennings, S. (1986c) 'The loneliness of the long distance therapist', paper presented to Jungian Summer Seminar, *British Journal of Psychotherapy*.

Jennings, S. (1986d) 'Metaphors of Violence', paper presented to International Congress of Group Psychotherapy, Zagreb.

Jennings, S. (ed) (1987) *Dramatherapy, Theory and Practice 1*. London: Routledge.

Jennings, S. (1990) *Dramatherapy with Families, Groups and Individuals*. London: Jessica Kingsley.

Jennings, S. (1992a) *Dramatherapy Theory and Practice 2*. London: Routledge.

Jennings, S. (1992b) 'The nature and scope of dramatherapy: theatre of healing.' In M. Cox (ed) *Shakespeare Comes to Broadmoor*. London: Jessica Kingsley.

Jennings, S. (1993) *Play Therapy with Children: A Practitioner's Guide*. Oxford: Blackwell Scientific.

Jennings, S. (1994) 'Unravelling dramatherapy: Ariadne's ball of thread.' *Family Context*.

Jennings, S. (1994) 'The theatre of healing: metaphor and metaphysics in the healing process.' In S. Jennings, A. Cattanach, S. Mitchell, A. Chesner and R. Meldrum (eds) *The Handbook of Dramatherapy*. London: Routledge.

Jennings, S. (ed) (1995a) *Infertility Counselling*. Oxford: Blackwell Science.

Jennings, S. (ed) (1995b) *Dramatherapy with Children and Adolescents*. London: Routledge.

Jennings, S. (1995c) *Theatre Ritual and Transformation*. London: Routledge.

Jennings, S. (ed) (1997) *Dramatherapy Theory and Practice 3*. London: Routledge.

Jennings, S. (in preparation) *The Theatres of Healing*. London: Jessica Kingsley Publishers.

Jennings, S. and Minde, A. (1994) *Art Therapy and Dramatherapy: Masks of The Soul*. London: Jessica Kingsley.

Jones, P. (1995) *Drama As Therapy: Theatre As Living*. London: Routledge.

Lahad, M. (1987/92) *Community Stress Prevention*. Israel: Kyriat Shmona.

Landy, R.J. (1986) *Drama Therapy, Concepts and Practices*. Chicago, Il: Charles C. Thomas.

Landy, R. (1993) *Persona and Performance – The Meaning of Role in Drama, Therapy and Everyday Life*. NY: Guilford and London: Jessica Kingsley.

Landy, R. (1996) *Essays in Drama Therapy: The Double Life*. London: Jessica Kingsley.

Langley, D.M. (1983) *Dramatherapy and Psychiatry*. London: Croom Helm.

Lewis, G. (1982) *Day of Shining Red*. Cambridge University Press.

Miller, A. (1990) *The Untouched Key*. London: Virago Press.

Mitchell, S. (ed) *Dramatherapy Clinical Studies*. London: Jessica Kingsley.

Moreno, J. (1947) *The Theatre of Spontaneity*. New York: Beacon House.

Napier, A. (1986) *Masks, Transformation and Paradox*. University of California Press.

Oaklander, V. (1978) *Windows to our Children*. Utah: Real People Press.

Radice, B. (1971) *Who's Who in the Ancient World*. Harmondsworth: Penguin.

Schechner, R. (1988) *Performance Theory*. New York: Routledge.

Showalter, E. (1985) 'Representing Ophelia: women, madness and the responsibilities of feminist criticism.' In P. Parker and G. Hartmann (eds) *Shakespeare and the Question of Theory*. New York: Methuen.

Slade, P. (1954) *Child Drama*. London: Hodder and Stoughton.

Stanislavski (1950/1981) *Building a Character*. London: Methuen.

Taplin, O. (1989) *Greek Fire*. London: Jonathan Cape.

Willett, J. (1964) *The Theatre of Bertold Brecht*. London: Methuen.

Wilshire, B. (1982) *Role Playing and Identity: The Limits of Theater as Metaphor*. Indiana University Press.

Winnicott, D.W. (1974) *Playing and Reality*. London: Pelican.

Index

Printed in the United States
92172LV00003B/307-318/A